"To read this highly ethnographic memoir of teaching English in the closed city of Luzhou in the 1980s is to have a window on the tensions and contradictions inherent in being a 'foreign expert' in a place both eager to engage the world and wary of doing so. Martens Friesen and Zehr approach their subject matter with humility and humor, thoughtfulness, and respect."

—LAURA HOSTETLER, professor of history and global Asian studies, University of Illinois at Chicago

"The authors provide a marvelous ringside seat to the efforts of two young American teachers in the 1980s to break down walls with students in China as the long-isolated country was beginning to open up to the outside world. Their moving stories are a reminder that people-to-people exchanges could again serve as a roadmap to boost connections between Chinese people and Americans today as suspicion and rivalry poison ties between Washington, DC, and Beijing."

—MURRAY HIEBERT, author of *Under Beijing's Shadow: Southeast Asia's China Challenge*

"As the only foreigners living in Luzhou during the 1980s, Martens Friesen and Zehr witnessed the initial, tentative opening of post-Maoist China. Along the way, their years there teaching English also opened doors in their own lives, revealing questions and possibilities of identity, faith, and friendship. In *Doors Cracked Open*, they offer the gift of stories—insightful, entertaining, vulnerable—of cross-cultural encounters and self-discovery."

—STEVEN M. NOLT, director, Young Center for Anabaptist and Pietist Studies, Elizabethtown College

"Animating this book is the authors' large-heartedness: large enough to encompass grace for their younger selves chafing against restrictions, and grace for their Chinese students, colleagues, and 'handlers' struggling to assess how quickly and far barriers to formerly forbidden connections with foreigners had been moved. Americanness and Chineseness undeniably shaped these encounters, but the real and timeless story is how forces like family, faith, and individual temperament determine the risks we take to understand and befriend each other."

—ANN MARTIN, former East Asia director, Mennonite Central Committee

Doors Cracked Open

Doors Cracked Open

Teaching in a Chinese Closed City

FRAN MARTENS FRIESEN
and MARY ANN ZEHR

Foreword by MYRRL BYLER

RESOURCE *Publications* · Eugene, Oregon

DOORS CRACKED OPEN
Teaching in a Chinese Closed City

Resource Publications
An Imprint of Wipf and Stock Publishers
199 W. 8th Ave., Suite 3
Eugene, OR 97401

www.wipfandstock.com

PAPERBACK ISBN: 978-1-6667-8880-8
HARDCOVER ISBN: 978-1-6667-8881-5
EBOOK ISBN: 978-1-6667-8882-2

From Fran
To my mom and dad, Phyllis and Elmer, who to me are the definition of hospitality that extends beyond boundaries.
Also, to my helpmeet, Ken, and my three beautiful adult children, Daniel, Loren, and Lan.

From Mary Ann

To my mother, Pearl

You modeled an approach to life of viewing anyone you meet, no matter who they are or where they are from, as a potential friend.

Table of Contents

Foreword

I FIRST READ *Doors Cracked Open: Teaching in a Chinese Closed City* at a time when there was a daily diet of negative news about China, and China's reporting on the United States was equally unfavorable. Tension between China and the West has ebbed and flowed for decades, but recent years have seen far too few serious attempts at finding common ground. Seemingly arbitrary or tit-for-tat government decisions have adversely affected educational and people-to-people exchanges, which have provided some balance and hope for more mutual understanding and trust between people with very different cultural traditions and histories.

Fran and Mary Ann have provided us with a personal window into the world of Chinese and American interaction during the 1980s, at a time when the doors in China had swung partially open and people from both China and the United States were attempting to gain some perspective on the other country. However, these two young American women did not live in Beijing or Shanghai or any of the other large Chinese cities that were quickly emerging from the dust of the past decades but were thrust into an isolated and "closed city" in China's southwestern Sichuan Province.

Foreigners received attention no matter where they were in China, but in cities like Luzhou, which had seen few if any foreigners for decades, the appearance of two young American women was eventful. Though respectful of school officials and the many rules they were asked to follow, Fran and Mary Ann also pushed the boundaries by developing friendships with their students and fellow teachers. Many foreigners in China during this time spent time only with other foreigners or complained bitterly about restrictions and cultural differences, but Fran and Mary Ann showed their hosts that they wanted to learn and engage with them as friends and fellow educators.

Through Fran and Mary Ann we meet students from a small and unimportant medical college, many who were not happy with the choice of a vocation foisted upon them by the social system. We feel their aspirations and hope for the future, but also their impatience with a system and families who remained traditional and seemingly stuck in the past. There is excitement about changes that are improving life but frustration with officials and leaders who seem to block their progress. For foreign teachers, there is much about life in China during the 1980s that does not make sense, cannot be understood, and raises innumerable unanswerable questions. Fran and Mary Ann describe how they found ways to fight the boredom, to build community, to create small moments of joy, and to laugh at themselves.

One of the first academic programs to begin after the doors to China opened, China Educational Exchange was a somewhat risky cooperative venture between Mennonite agencies and colleges and educational institutions in Sichuan Province. Fran and Mary Ann were representative of many of the teachers who were part of the program, dedicated members of their small denomination with a desire to serve and learn overseas, despite the many challenges. Through the stories and experiences they share, we understand how their strong family and religious background helped them to not only survive the isolation and constant supervision, but also thrive as individuals when many would have simply given up. They and the program they represented were open about their Christian faith and background, but also upfront about how they understood the damage done to the Chinese people by Western and Japanese colonial powers and the negative association with Christianity.

As the relationship between China and the United States continues to face strong challenges, Fran and Mary Ann provide an example of how cultural differences, suspicion, and distrust can be overcome. There is a willingness to give the other the benefit of the doubt, to work hard at seeing the other's perspective and to recognize what everyone has in common. They avoid viewing China through rose-colored glasses, but perhaps more importantly, they refuse to adopt the critical and condescending attitude that often characterizes writing about China by outsiders. Instead, they provide a more objective perspective on how developing relationships across major cultural, historical, and political chasms is difficult but rewarding work.

Myrrl Byler
PhD in Intercultural Studies
Director of China Educational Exchange/
Mennonite Partners in China, 1990–2020

Acknowledgments

THIS MEMOIR WOULD NOT have come to be if our Chinese students and colleagues had not taken risks in the 1980s to tell us their stories and talk about their society with us. To the people of Luzhou, we acknowledge that authentic interactions with you transformed us and gave us a story to tell. We are indebted to you.

Though nearly four decades have passed since we lived in Luzhou, we are aware that some of the people we interacted with still face security risks. Therefore, we have changed your names, not identified you in photos, and left out details from conversations.

We didn't change the name of a prominent Luzhou Medical College leader, Teacher Lin. He was such an important person in the foreign affairs office that changing his name wouldn't provide identity protection. Teacher Lin is also no longer in this world; he passed away in 2006. We also didn't change the names of Chinese graduate students at Indiana University, Bloomington, who were interviewed by Mary Ann and whose names were published in *The Indianapolis Star* in 1989.

We thank Myrrl Byler, the director of China Educational Exchange/ Mennonite Partners in Education from 1990-2020, for sending us organizational documents, some of which we had never laid eyes on. Those documents helped us to gain a deeper understanding of perspectives of China Educational Exchange and medical college leaders in the 1980s. We are also grateful to you, Myrrl, for sharing your take on our experiences in a foreword to our memoir.

We are grateful to the people who read drafts of our memoir: Cynthia Yoder, Joy Versluis, Rosalyn Myers Kniss, and Hope Nisly. Your thoughtful reading of the book and comments helped us to greatly improve it. Daniel Friesen, thank you for your insight that led us to frame the memoir to better engage readers.

We appreciate how Kathleen Weaver Kurtz, who had published a memoir with Wipf and Stock, advised us on how to effectively work with the publisher. We appreciate Joanie Eppinga for carefully reading and co-pyediting our book.

We are indebted to Ken Friesen for encouraging us to continue on in our writing. We also thank him for creating a map of China that shows cities that we visited and for helping with technical issues, such as digitally converting our photos.

We both acknowledge the wonderful support and continued interest from friends and family as we shared with them the ups and downs of writing a memoir. We needed and appreciated your encouragement. Thank you.

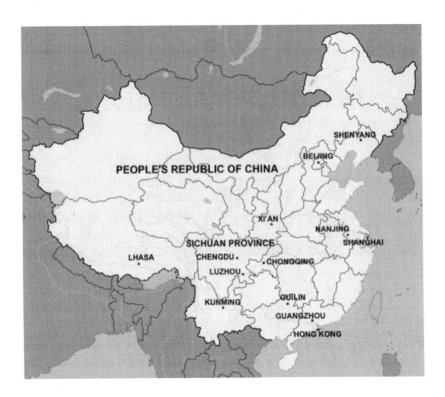

1

Luzhou City through a Modern Lens

Fran

ON THE TRAIN TO the city of Luzhou in Sichuan, China, I became fidgety. I was not sure what I would encounter in the next few hours. It had been thirty-one years since I had last seen this midsize town on the banks of the Yangtze River. Then I was in my mid-20s, single, trying out teaching abroad for the first time, separated for two years from everything and everyone I had known. Everyone, that is, except for my college friend Mary Ann with whom I had agreed to teach English. We were placed in a Chinese medical school located in the hinterlands of Sichuan, near the Yangtze River, far from any other foreigner. It was just the two of us Americans in a sea of four hundred thousand Chinese people. We had joked that we were part of a great sociological experiment. And so we were, in some ways.

The train stopped at the station in Luzhou exactly on time. It was a high-speed train, hurtling us from Chengdu to Luzhou in less than four hours. I recalled arduous eight-hour trips always tinged with the smell of gasoline—that was if the bus did not break down or stop for an accident. I stepped off the train, feeling light, unencumbered by the suitcases and boxes that I had come with some thirty years earlier. I still feel embarrassed when I think of the blue-uniformed workers straining under the weight of all the things we young women felt we could not do without for two years.

Now in 2019, my husband and two young adult children were in China with a group of students from our California university on a learning tour. The fact that the place where I had spent two formative years was just "down the road" from Chengdu, Sichuan, where we were staying, was too tempting to pass up. The leader of our tour group arranged for a woman he worked with to meet us at the train station outside of Luzhou and drive us around for the day. Teacher Wang actually worked at the same institution where I had taught in Luzhou, a wonderful coincidence.

Teacher Wang, a smiling middle-aged woman, surprised us by pulling up in her own car, a nice-looking Hyundai. A college teacher driving? Her own car, no less? In my previous experience in Luzhou, I had been used to paid drivers, military-trained, driving black, family-size Russian Volgas.

As we pulled into town, I strained to catch glimpses of familiar landmarks. The narrow, crowded streets filled with tea shops and pedestrians, the monstrous cement department stores, the city park with its many steps. I saw nothing that looked familiar. The city I had known was completely changed, as if it had never been. In its stead were glass-fronted, multiple-storied buildings, car showrooms, wide boulevards, median strips of grass and flowers, even—gasp—a Starbucks and a McDonald's. Teacher Wang drove us over the shimmering bridge with white columns, and suddenly we were at the college gates.

For the first time, I felt the familiar wash over me. The gate was the same, with its little guardhouse on one side and a large arched sign that proclaimed, in red Chinese script, "Luzhou Medical College." I got out of the car a bit apprehensively, expecting to see a formal delegation ready to usher us up the wide cement ramp flanked by camphor trees on both sides. I had not formally warned the school that I was coming, as I wished to avoid the formal and awkward welcome tea, followed by meetings, agendas, and a banquet weighed down with toasts and speeches. I wanted to sneak in, as incognito as possible, show my family around, and sneak back out again.

I glanced around as I stood at the entrance. The entrance to what? What was I expecting? What would I find here? Not far from the front of my mind loomed some cloudy thoughts. Memories of media images of the tragedies at Tiananmen Square when student protestors for democracy were gunned down, about a year and a half after I left China. Thoughts of how tensions between U.S. and Chinese government leaders had put a damper on plans for Western students to live and study in China and for Chinese students to study in the United States. Now, walking up the broad entrance, was I to see just a shadow of our former life? What about my students? Would anyone remember the two years I had been here? Would anyone care? I took a deep breath, taking the first step up the familiar 220-step mossy stairway rising into the trees and hazy sky.

2

The Backstory: Mennonites in Sichuan

Mary Ann

CHINA HAD WHAT WAS called an open-door policy to the West, spearhead-
ed by China's paramount leader, Deng Xiaoping, in the 1980s. That "open
door"—perhaps more accurately characterized as a "cracked door"—made
it possible for Fran and me to be teachers in China. I taught in China from
August 1985 to June 1987. Fran started her two-year term a half year after
I did and stayed until the beginning of 1988.

We were in China, and particularly in Sichuan Province, because we
were Mennonites. J. Lawrence Burkholder, a Mennonite theologian, and
his wife, Harriet, had created the connections between North American
Mennonites and government and higher education leaders in Sichuan that
enabled Fran and me to be in the country. J. Lawrence Burkholder was
president of Goshen College, a Mennonite college in Indiana, from 1971
to 1984. His term overlapped with the time we were students in Goshen.

Mennonites are members of a Christian body recognized by the U.S.
government as a "historic peace church." Their pacifist position has caused
them at times to treat boundaries and politics between countries as more
fluid than other people might. It has sometimes led Mennonites to engage
in humanitarian efforts in countries that are considered to be antagonistic
to the United States.

Back in the 1940s, Burkholder had worked for the nonprofit development organizations Mennonite Central Committee and Church World
Service, flying freight planes and coordinating relief supplies in China. He

and his family, who were based in Shanghai, were evacuated from China to the United States about six months before Communists took control of the city in May 1949.[1]

For decades, it wasn't safe for Chinese people to be in contact with any Americans. During the Cultural Revolution in China (1966–1976), groups of young people called Red Guards beat up and sometimes killed Chinese people who were associated with Western ideas or traditional Chinese culture. Many people perceived to have had connections to Western culture—such as foreign-language teachers, musicians who played Western music, or people who had associated with Christian missionaries—were imprisoned.

However, in the 1970s, the xenophobia of some Chinese people toward Westerners was easing up. Burkholder had a chance to tour China in 1975 with a group of educators. He was clearly impressed by some of the changes in the country since the 1949 Communist Revolution, led by Mao Zedong (Chairman Mao). Chinese people called the takeover by Communists "Liberation."

Burkholder thought it was remarkable that China had found a way to feed its people. He recalled seeing refugees in the 1940s who were thin and sickly for lack of food. He observed that, by contrast, in the New China, everyone received rations of rice, vegetables, and even chicken or duck.[2] Also, Burkholder observed values practiced by Chinese people that overlapped with Mennonite values and resonated with him. For instance, he observed that the government leaders had organized Chinese society so that people could serve others. Some 400 million young people had been taught to do so. [3] The idea of serving others is also prevalent in Mennonite circles, so this mandate stood out to him. Burkholder also praised Chinese society for an emphasis on simplicity, another value that Mennonites hold dear. He noted that the New China didn't have private cars, private estates, night clubs, or jewelry. He said the country was free of advertising agents, athletic stars, and film celebrities.[4]

In 1979, the Burkholders were guests of Sichuan Normal University in Chengdu, China. During their visit, Burkholder proposed a student exchange on the spot, worked out the details with government officials, and

1. Burkholder, *Recollections*, 95.
2. Burkholder, "Rethinking Christian Life," 211.
3. Burkholder, "Rethinking Christian Life," 209.
4. Burkholder, "Rethinking Christian Life," 212–13.

had it approved in just a few days.[5] It was an act of diplomacy that amazed China watchers. Consequently, in 1980, twenty Goshen College students studied at Sichuan Normal University for a semester. At the same time, a group of nine Chinese professors from Sichuan colleges traveled to Goshen and studied there for a full academic year.

Back in the United States, the China student-scholar exchange created a buzz on the campus of Goshen College, where Fran and I were then students. We both noticed how groups of American students who returned from studying in China were close-knit and applied their China experience to various endeavors, such as art or poetry. They tended to be some of the most intellectually curious students on campus. A few of the students who had been to China traipsed around campus in padded olive-green Mao coats.

Soon five Mennonite agencies collaborated to form China Educational Exchange (CEE), which would send teachers to China and also support opportunities for Chinese educators to study at Mennonite colleges in the United States. CEE, based in Winnipeg, Canada, assigned its first teachers to Sichuan Normal University in 1981. That was twelve years before the United States Peace Corps started its China program.[6] One Peace Corps English teacher, Peter Hessler, made himself and the Sichuan backwater city of Fuling world famous in his 2001 book, *River Town: Two Years on the Yangtze.*

During 2020, both CEE (which in 2006 was renamed Mennonite Partners in China) and the Peace Corps ended their decades-long programs in China. For Mennonite Partners in China, the change was due to budget cuts related to the global coronavirus pandemic. For the Peace Corps, according to a 2020 article penned by Hessler in the *New Yorker*, it was because of pressure from growing anti-China sentiment in the United States. The Trump Administration's decision to end the program was made in a closed-door meeting of the National Security Council.[7]

꿍

I was one of three CEE English teachers assigned to Sichuan Normal University in August 1985. But after that first half year in China, I

5. Burkholder, *Recollections*, 179.

6. Hessler, "The Peace Corps," para. 1.

7. Hessler, "The Peace Corps," paras. 40–41.

transferred to Luzhou—a new location for CEE—because Fran was coming to China and CEE had decided to place the two of us there. I wrote to her, "I think, friend, that we are going to be isolated, isolated. I'm a little frightened to move when everything is going so well here in Chengdu, but I'm also willing to try something new."

During a two-day visit to Luzhou Medical College in October 1985, Bert Lobe, director of CEE, had made a point to college officials that they were working with a Mennonite organization. Bert was impressed by the deputy director of the college's foreign affairs office, who was called Teacher Lin. He had completed a master's degree program in linguistics at Ohio State University the previous year. During Bert's visit, Teacher Lin made an effort to learn something about the Mennonites. Bert wrote in a CEE report:

> I indicated how important it is for them to understand clearly who we are. The next morning following this discussion, the Ohio graduate came to me and commented: "I consulted my dictionary on Mennonites. You have a leader; his name is Menno Simons. Your religion forbids going to war, the use of force, and empha- sizes simple living. It also forbids the swearing of oaths. Is that right? This is what I found. I will pass this information to my col- leagues. Is it true?"[8]

Fran and I were evolving to be Christians interested in social justice who wanted to facilitate global connections between people. I was in a questioning phase of my faith; Fran's faith was on steadier footing. We were open to talking about religion with people who brought it up with us, but neither of us expected Chinese people to become Christians because of interactions with us. We were young and single—I was 23, Fran 24—and we sought adventure through teaching and travel. Luzhou Medical College agreed to accept us as teachers and provide us with room and board plus an allowance of about $100 per month in Chinese currency, *renminbi*. That would more than adequately cover our needs.

As it turned out, we lived in China at a unique time, when our Chinese colleagues and students were recovering from the turbulence and unpre- dictability of the Cultural Revolution. Some Chinese people we met were tentatively trusting that China's leaders were serious about opening their country up to the world and embraced the presence of American teachers

8. "Summary of Visit," 2.

such as Fran and me as a symbol of positive change. Others, scarred by the Cultural Revolution, understandably kept their distance from us.

In late 1986, during our stint in China, students on the east coast of the country held protests calling for "freedom" and "democracy," a movement that would gain momentum and erupt in the occupation of Tiananmen Square by university students in China's capital of Beijing, starting in April 1989. Western China scholars have called the Tiananmen student protests "a revolution of popular expectations."[9] It wasn't long after Fran and I had returned to the United States that the Chinese government sent the message that it would tolerate only so much openness. The government ordered tanks into Tiananmen Square, killing hundreds of students on June 4, 1989, in a move that shocked the world.

9. Davis and Vogel, "Introduction," 2.

PART I:
Into the Unknown

3

First Impressions of Luzhou

FRAN

Luzhou city nestled between the Yangtze and Tuo rivers

MARY ANN AND I first met at Goshen College at an orientation for the college's study abroad program. Virtually every student at Goshen was required to live, study, and work in a country outside of the United States in order to graduate.

I had been intrigued by the newly established China study program and had signed up for it, but my name had been put on a waiting list.

Disappointed, I decided to go to Honduras instead. So did Mary Ann, a dark-haired woman with intense blue eyes. We clicked right away. In the capital city of Honduras, Tegucigalpa, we often went out to lunch together in between language and culture classes. At a final gathering of Goshen College students back in the capital after our work assignments, Mary Ann and I decided to keep in touch.

So it was that in the summer of 1985 we made the decision to embark on another international adventure together, this time to China. I had just finished a grueling year as a teacher in Boston. Moreover, my boyfriend, Ken Friesen, had just decided he wanted to go for a three-year service term to Lesotho, Africa. I was rather taken aback by that decision which then prodded me to go on my own adventure. In a letter to Mary Ann I wrote, "Although I am excited for him . . . I also am hesitant because that will probably call a halt to our relationship. But we are still young, yes? We must fly our wings before they become too droopy with age!"

Mary Ann had been working as an editorial assistant in a textbook publishing company in Manhattan. Despite the excitement of living in vibrant big cities, both of us had felt a restlessness and dissatisfaction with our jobs. I had heard about a call from China Educational Exchange for volunteer teachers. I immediately contacted the only person I could think of who would be crazy enough to go to China with me: Mary Ann. In my application to CEE, I wrote, "We [Mary Ann and I] have found from the past experience in Honduras that we work together in an excellent way to push each other into concerted efforts to interact with the culture." And so we went.

Despite all the well-laid plans, we could not imagine what we were in for, the deep joys and challenges ahead. But we got an inkling of the intensity of the experience when we stepped foot on the campus of Luzhou Medical College for the first time together on February 20, 1986. The first surprise was our living space. Initially we had been promised a spot in the English teachers' dormitory (there were Chinese English teachers living on campus as well). We had thought this would provide a ready-made community. However, that is not where we were put up. We walked into a pleasantly shaded courtyard and up to the green door in the middle of two other apartments on either side of us. Our neighbors, we found out, were the family of a retired Communist Party secretary on one side and a retired Luzhou Medical School president on the other. In other words, we knew we had been set apart and expected to be on our best behavior.

We hardly had time to settle in when we were summoned to a welcoming banquet. Banquets were something altogether outside our experience, an intricate dance of exotic dishes, brought in and announced one by one—tortoise, sea cucumbers, and rabbit—interspersed with constant toasts of one kind or another, for which we had to raise our glasses and down a throat-burning gulp of the famous Luzhou *baijiu* (rice wine) that tasted to us like kerosene.

Luzhou was famous throughout China for its excellent rice wine, estimated to be about 60 percent proof. It was so strong that people drank it in thimble-sized porcelain shot glasses. Rice wine was served for every banquet, which was any time someone of importance stepped onto campus, whether a Chinese person or foreigner. At the many subsequent banquets we attended in Luzhou, we found that we could handle only a couple of shots at a time.

That evening, Mary Ann and I squirmed under the constant attention, with people peppering us with questions and filling our bowls in proper hosting style (though sometimes with things we would rather not eat). We were the subjects of grand toasts. At one point, as I ventured to take a sip of the rice wine on the table in front of me, I found the whole group standing and raising their glasses. Apparently, in China, one usually drinks wine in conjunction with a toast! I hurriedly stood and stammered out, "To the friendship of our two countries!" (a standard line I had heard). We all drank and sat down.

Another faux pas was when we failed a trick question—"Would you like some rice?"—put to us at the end of a long meal filled with items we did not recognize. A bit of bland and familiar food sounded good to us at the moment, so we said yes. As we learned later, this was not the right response; this means the guest did not get enough food to eat during the banquet and thus had to "fill up" on the everyday food of rice, with the host thereby disgraced! This mistake was not the only one we would make during that first week and beyond. Fortunately for us, the school officials were quick to forgive the young and inexperienced Americans with rude manners.

As we stretched out on one of our beds that night, trying to digest all the unfamiliar foods and processing the evening's events, we realized that we were going to need each other on a much deeper level than we had anticipated, that we were each other's sounding board and a way to remind ourselves that we were okay in this strange and unpredictable world. Nevertheless, we wondered, how would our friendship survive under so much pressure?

4

Lockdown

Mary Ann

The global pandemic that began in 2020 forced many people to learn what it means to be socially isolated for an extended period. But in 1986, when Fran and I began our teaching assignment in Luzhou, we were clueless about what the separation from the social and cultural interactions we were accustomed to would mean. Fran wrote just before she arrived in China:

> Sometimes I fear a little for the time away under such circumstances (no foreign teachers in Luzhou other than Mary Ann and I). But I will look at each semester and stop thinking, "Two years! Oh my gosh!" I believe this experience will make me a more flexible person, also more disciplined and studious. I have not been that way since college really. There really won't be a lot of diversions, as I gather, although I really do like Chinese music—at least some of it . . . Well, I really want to give appreciation for this venture—it is crazy in many ways. I am sure I don't know the half of it yet.

After we set foot in Luzhou in February 1986, Fran and I were the only two foreigners living in this city at the confluence of the Yangtze River and the Tuo River. Luzhou was a "closed city." That meant foreigners needed official government permission to live there. The city was closed to foreign tourists. We and the CEE leaders didn't know the day-to-day life implications of what it meant to live in a "closed city." We gradually realized that we were not trusted by our hosts to move about and interact with everyone freely.

The 1984 Lonely Planet guidebook for China listed only twenty-nine Chinese cities where foreign tourists could go and stay overnight without a permit. Another one hundred or so places were "open" to foreign tourists if they got a travel permit from the Public Security Bureau, or police.[1] In the mid-1980s, China was continually adding to its list of cities "open" to foreign tourism.

Luzhou was decreed "open" in October 1986. That change in status made a difference in that we were allowed to visit restaurants and movie theaters. But that change of status had little impact on how our interactions with our students and colleagues were managed, a situation that did not fluctuate a lot during the time we lived in Luzhou.

Politically ambitious Chinese leaders and Communist Party members of Luzhou Medical College restricted our freedom with an approach that had been common in the late 1970s, right after the end of the Cultural Revolution, but was not common in the 1980s. The other teachers we knew living in Sichuan told us they were less closely monitored and had more freedom than we did to explore their physical environment and interact with Chinese people. I dubbed our situation a "social moratorium." But at least Fran and I had each other. My paternal grandma recognized that, telling me in a letter, "You have your dear Fran with you."

When we agreed to work in a "closed city," we knew that foreigners could not just casually pass through the city. As recently as 1984, Kathleen Griffin, who had been born in Luzhou to Canadian Methodist missionaries, had tried to visit Luzhou while traveling in China with a tour group. She came only as close as Chengdu and was not permitted to see Luzhou because of its "closed" status.

We learned about the missionary presence of Griffin's family in Luzhou because Griffin wrote personal letters to Fran inquiring about our lives in the city after we began teaching there. Her family had left Luzhou for Canada in 1926, never to return. Griffin's 1986 letters mentioned the evangelical work of her father, J. M. Would. He had been in charge of two street chapels in the city, but he was more focused on converting Chinese people in the countryside. In his eyes, Luzhou was a city of sin. Would wrote in a 1920 mission report:

1. Samagalski and Buckley, *China: A Travel Survival Kit*, 92.

In this country district there are approximately four hundred thousand people. We as a Mission are responsible for their evangelization, and at the present time I am the only foreign missionary working among them. As in Christian lands, so here in China, most of our promising boys are from the homes of the country. The city is the centre of vice and degradation.[2]

Griffin apparently had a different view of Luzhou than her father. She described city scenes fondly and longed her whole life to revisit the city. Years later, we learned that after her family had left, other Canadian Methodist missionaries had continued working in Luzhou, at least up through the early 1940s.[3] China expelled all missionaries in 1951.

Luzhou had received some Westerners not long before Fran and I moved there. Starting in 1974, some Americans and other Westerners had helped to build a chemical plant fueled by Luzhou's abundant natural gas. We didn't know how long they had stayed in the city for this purpose. Teacher Lin, the same man who had been part of the negotiations to host Fran and me as teachers and who managed our lives and work, had served the Westerners as an interpreter. He said the Western consultants had been much more restricted than we were. He implied that it hadn't bothered them. At the same time, Teacher Lin acknowledged that the Americans stationed in Luzhou in the 1970s were "very bad-tempered" at times. The American consulate general in Chengdu had told me they had balked at the heavy restrictions.

During my six months in Chengdu, before moving to Luzhou, I had moved freely about the city. I wasn't aware that anyone paid much attention to my social interactions with Chinese people my own age. I'd once spent half a day with a male student my age, biking around the city and visiting a Buddhist temple. No one had raised an eyebrow. Another student had hosted me and two other foreign teachers in his home for a Spring Festival banquet and had taken us to see a lantern festival. No special permission from officials at Sichuan Normal University had been required.

Luzhou Medical College leaders had invited us to live on campus to teach English—merely that. We were charged with creating and running a full-time intensive English course for about thirty health professionals each semester. Apparently, the leaders didn't want us to spread Western ideas to

2. Missionary Society of the Methodist Church, *Our West China Mission*, 220.

3. Song, "A Study of Three Women," 97–98. From 1940 through 1942, Grace and Roy Webster, sent by the Canadian Methodist Mission, lived in Luzhou.

students or others in a way that they perceived as being akin to an ideological virus. They seemed to think they could crack open a door and not let any flies in. Actually, little did they know we were not good candidates for spreading ideas about popular North American culture or politics. We had both been raised in Mennonite families in a rather sheltered way. Our families stressed Mennonite values of simplicity and nonmaterialism. We would not be very good at spreading capitalism.

Nevertheless, we were banned for months from participating in any "unofficial activities," social events that weren't approved by the foreign affairs office, or *waiban*. For two and a half months—from the third week of February through the first week of May—we couldn't leave the Luzhou Medical College campus, even to go to the post office, without a Chinese escort. In May, the *waiban* decided we could leave campus on our own, but only for the purpose of mailing letters in town. No one specified that we had to take a direct route, so we began to explore the city on foot by taking circuitous routes to the post office. In time, the official word from the *waiban* was that we could take walks in Luzhou City as long as we "stayed inside the rivers." Oh, did we ever take advantage of that leeway!

§

Why didn't we openly defy the rules? The rules were intended to keep us from getting close to people, and we had come this long way because we wanted to make friends with Chinese people. We wouldn't be able to do that without intermingling with students and teaching colleagues. We soon realized that when we broke the rules in our interactions with people, our potential Chinese friends got in trouble. It was disheartening to hear they had been criticized in political meetings for socializing with us without permission. We didn't want to jeopardize any opportunities for them. Also, we wanted to know more about Luzhou. We were guests. We didn't want to get kicked out of the city. The Communist Party leaders or hardliners sprinkled among our students could turn against us in a heartbeat, and our adventure in a "closed city" would be over. Therefore, we focused on navigating around restrictions, not defying them.

Restrictions on our interactions with anyone besides each other became evident right away. From the start we were assigned an interpreter—Teacher Luo—who was charged with minding our affairs.

The day after we arrived, Teacher Luo took us on a walking tour of the city. I ran into one of my former students from Chengdu and her mother in the street. We were thrilled to see each other, and she promptly invited me to visit her home. She said she would come for me at 7 p.m., and she was true to her word.

Teacher Luo suggested we talk in the tearoom on the first floor of our quarters, but this student had been to my apartment in Chengdu, so I invited her to my bedroom. Teacher Luo invited herself upstairs with us and sat knitting as we talked. The young woman stayed a couple of hours. She never mentioned the invitation she'd so eagerly offered previously to receive me in her home, the kind of hospitality I'd experienced already from students in Chengdu, so I didn't mention it. As I said goodbye to her at the door, she took my arm and said: "I'm so sorry, but there are many reasons why I cannot take you to my home. My parents are really grateful that you taught me English. I cannot receive you in my home. Maybe you understand."

"I understand," I said. "Sometimes it is difficult to invite someone from another country to your house."

"Yes," she said.

This was the first of many rescinded invitations.

১৬৩

Hu Bing was the first student in our intensive English class to invite us to his home. It was an apartment in the six-story building for medical school teachers across from our building. He was a few years older than we were, married and with a family. We had caught a glimpse of his slender, fine-featured wife on a balcony, holding a chubby infant. He wanted us to meet his family. Later, with disappointment, Hu Bing took back the invitation, explaining that the *waiban* had told him he wasn't allowed to host us in his apartment.

At the end of March, we were delighted that the students in the intensive English class had an idea for an outing. They asked us to accompany them to watch a soccer match at a chemical college, a ten-minute bus ride away. One of our students was going to be playing. The person most responsible for us on campus, Teacher Lin, called the *waiban* of the city of Luzhou and then reported that the city officials had said we couldn't go. A couple of the students showed their frustration. "Too many regulations," one muttered.

Director Yin (left) and Teacher Lin (right), the top two officials of the Luzhou Medical College *waiban,* on a ferry at Dragon Horse Lake

As a substitute for the soccer game plan, the college leaders took Fran and me by car to visit nearby Dragon Horse Lake. Teacher Lin and another official from the *waiban,* Director Yin, toted bags of chocolate, oranges, soft drinks, and candy for us. Teacher Luo came along. The park manager arranged for us to be paddled around with the leaders in a fancy little ferry. We drank tea on the boat and peered out of its windows at schoolchildren rowing on the lake. The children were curious and swarmed around us when we landed. I saw a playful side of Teacher Luo there. She jumped from one human-made concrete stepping stone to another in the lake. And Teacher Lin sang a song he'd picked up in English: "Row, Row, Row Your Boat," but he put his own twist on the ending, "Life is but a dream—or is it?"

༄

I had received a language lesson from the outing, picking up the Chinese words for "bamboo," "rowing a boat," and "bridge." We found that when we learned a few words and used them, people could understand them and were pleased, so that stoked our motivation to learn more Chinese.

The school leaders continued to take us to events or on field trips on weekends. Middle-aged men in dark blazers and dress slacks accompanied two smiley young teachers wearing jeans and light sweaters or rumpled dresses pulled out of the suitcases kept under beds. We didn't have closets or dressers. We appreciated the efforts of the *waiban* officials to entertain us, but Fran and I longed for friendships with Chinese people our own age.

It didn't take long to deduce that the *waiban* permitted only some people—those who were middle-aged or well-connected politically—to host us in their private homes. The leaders didn't tell us directly we couldn't visit the homes of students our age. Rather, they told our students they couldn't receive us in their homes; students knew it was risky politically for them to break the rules.

Although the college leaders made a point of preventing close personal friendships, they supported us in practicing English conversation with groups of students. We couldn't go to students' homes, but they could come to ours. We established a routine of hosting our students in weekly tea parties for "English practice" and didn't run up against any obstacles. The leaders didn't seem to mind if we became friends with our students in groups each semester. That was the way to go.

A Lockdown Timeline

Fran

March 1986: I wrote, "There are no expats here, but the staring isn't as bad as I thought. I don't feel too isolated yet."

April 1986: Our CEE friends come from Chongqing, the first time we have seen foreigners in two months.

April 1986: I wrote, "Anyone who comes to visit must first ask permission of the leaders. We DO invite five-six students to our place every Saturday night."

September 1986: There are restrictions on our informal activities with former students, e.g. cooking lessons. I wrote, "Why? It seems we are to be teaching-machines, not people who make intimate friendships with Chinese people. All so confusing. Perhaps we will protest this and see if we can change some policies."

October 1986: Luzhou becomes an open city. Not long afterward, we get official permission to visit restaurants and go to movies in Luzhou.

February 1987: I wrote, "Today's big feat was venturing out to a local restaurant and eating *jiaozi* dumplings. Really good—one of the first times we have gone out alone."

June 1987: We go to a young teacher's house for dinner (she was married to a city official); we go over at 3 p.m. and eat at 8:30 p.m. We watch and help cook: fried eggplant stuffed with pork, bamboo shoot soup, fried catfish.

I wrote, "Students are so sweet sometimes! . . . One student told me I really couldn't learn China unless I lived in the home of a Chinese family—I said I would if I could. Oh, would I!"

5

Scenes from Luzhou

FRAN

OUR COLLEGE ON ZHONG Mountain retained some of the peaceful atmosphere of its Buddhist temple roots. In fact, the campus movie house was a replica of a Ming Dynasty temple. There were steps, trees, gargoyles, stone pillars, rock gardens, winding paths. Students and doctors walked around in white cloaks, sometimes hanging on each other as they went to

Luzhou Medical College campus, site of a former Buddhist temple

22

classrooms, the dining room, and the hospitals. There were two hospital buildings, one for Western medicine and one for Eastern medicine; the latter used acupuncture and had bins of various traditional medicinal herbs.

Our apartment was at the very top of the mountain. We found out later that we had been given VIP accommodations, situated as we were between college leaders. On the first floor was our cozy little tearoom, complete with a small fridge (a rarity at the time when most Chinese people had iceboxes), a faux-leather couch, two armchairs, a phone for calling out (another rarity), and a balcony that overlooked a small courtyard. It did take some getting used to in terms of colors—red carpet, blue walls, pastel-green window trim! After going up the cement stairs, we came out on a hallway. To the left was a porcelain counter with a single burner and a teakettle. Up above the counter was a small gas water heater, which we had to light (a scary experience, as it would poof in a burst of flame) to have hot water for a shower in the adjacent bathroom. We were very pleased to see a Western toilet, a bathtub/shower combination, nicely tiled floor, and a small window that featured the scenic side of the building with a forest of camphor trees on the steep mountain slope.

To the right of the staircase was my bedroom, a large room with the same red carpet as downstairs and a two-toned wall—blue on the bottom half and white on the top half. My balcony faced the courtyard. Next to my bedroom was Mary Ann's. Her desk faced out the window to the view of trees. To the left of the desk was a door that led out to the balcony, the one we retreated to when we needed a measure of isolation and relaxation. The air was fresh, and it was fairly quiet, except that TVs often blared late at night. On a very rare clear day, we could see the rivers curving and shining in the city far below.

The courtyard was our window into the lives of our immediate neighbors. It was the place where our neighbors' children played, the elderly rested, and people conversed. I often looked out to see what was going on in the outside world. Sometimes I saw little children riding around on tricycles; one time I saw and heard workers twanging cotton on a wire-frame bed, making filling for comforters.

In those early days of getting used to Luzhou life, as Mennonite women raised up on the principle of simple living, we often felt uneasy about all the extra comforts and special treatment. We had two house workers who came daily to briefly clean our rooms. We did not eat with the Chinese staff or students either—which was also true of the twenty-some CEE teachers whom we met up with during our travels on school breaks. Mary Ann and

I walked into a separate room in the dining hall with one round table for us, and a young woman brought in our food. I wrote to my parents, "Obviously, you can see that they treat us like queens."

Men fluff cotton for a comforter in our courtyard. Our apartment is on the right.

Getting special meals cooked for us, having fish nearly every day (and even rabbit one day), and being hosted with fancy banquets when our leaders came seemed rather extravagant to us, and we felt a bit ashamed of all the attention. But what could we do? It was our host's way of showing hospitality.

When we eventually got permission to walk on our own in the town, I wrote a thorough description of what I saw:

> The streets down in the town are dust-covered. So is everything else: dust-covered stalls, dust-covered goods, dust-covered open-air restaurants. When it rains, the dust turns to mud. Small shops line narrow streets. People carry string bags bulging with the day's bargains—oranges, celery, cabbage, green onions, apples, mushrooms, bamboo and lotus shoots. A duck sits passively scrunched up in a bag. Some hold chickens upside down or maybe even a dead, skinned rabbit. In the meat section of the free market, fifty or more ducks are tied together by the feet and sprawled all over

the cement, honking occasionally but generally trying to maintain some dignity in their awkward positions. Duck feathers are strewn all over the walkway—out in the sun to dry.

Further down, eel is being skinned—basins are ready to catch the inordinate amount of blood from each one. Bored clerks sleep, heads down at the checkout counter of department stores, lights dimmed or off entirely. They are paid by the state, the proverbial "iron-rice bowl" so there are few incentives to be very productive.

Some ancient-looking men with beards gather around a small table, wearing huge Mao coats and Russian-looking fur caps, playing cards. A child is being given a bath in a small wooden tub right in the street. A crowd gathers around a storyteller, banging his gong, making his monkey do flips and tricks, and then asking for money. Strange-looking buses honk their way by—black tarp-like bags filled with natural gas on the top.

A little girl with bright red bows in her hair and two red dots on her cheek and forehead (a sign of beauty for children) swings by. Couples, walking close but never touching, walk past in latest fashions—this year it is trench coats, jeans, and Shanghai sweaters. A man walks by with a pole over his shoulders and two buckets of slop; we hold our noses. People browse at a private book collection set up on the sidewalk. They are charged a few cents an hour to read there.

A team of men heave a cart full of heavy cement slabs, brick, or coal on up the hill—they're part of a manual labor team, building new roads and widening old ones in Luzhou. Construction is accomplished largely by hand and with many, many workers. The workers often labor all night, tearing down scaffolds and throwing the long steel parts down like huge javelins—it's noisy and dangerous if one doesn't keep alert! There are so few safety precautions; torch-work that is so blindingly bright is done without any face protection or glasses.

Every time Mary Ann and I went out, curious townspeople stared; when we stopped to look at something or to bargain for vegetables or tasty tangerines, we invariably drew a crowd. And when we went out walking, we never knew quite what to expect: a man watering ducks as they walked down the hilly street, someone hauling a dresser on his back, women picking lice out of each other's hair. As we gradually were allowed more freedom to roam the city, we began enjoying the longer strolls into town. We discovered there were different sections. For example, there was the fishing area, which was for those of a lower class but in a clean, old section of town with steps leading down to the river. Some of these people actually lived on the boats, which were moored on the banks of the Yangtze at night. We once were astonished to see the boatmen gathered in one boat, sitting on stools and watching TV on the deck! It seemed quite a nomadic life—little junks, naked children, and a small hollow inside for sleeping, with cooking facilities out the back.

Another sector we stumbled on was the rich neighborhood (there were such distinctions of class—not quite so obvious but existent still): a motor-cycle on the patio, freshly painted buildings, rooms that were small but well kept up, wide boulevards with flowers planted in islands in the middle. This nice part of town was so different from the crowded downtown markets with hawkers and peasants calling out to sell their piles of vegetables and fruits while holding small hand scales to measure *jin* (pounds).

One day we saw a woman who had just fallen from a second-story window—out cold. We sometimes saw patients carried by two or four people on makeshift stretchers over the heads of the passersby—that sight felt like an older China—such a strange mixture of old and new.

6

Eager Students

MARY ANN

Our first intensive English class at Luzhou Medical College

TEACHING IN LUZHOU WAS fun. True to the agreement forged by our organization with the college, we were assigned only one class of about thirty students each semester for intensive English. We each taught the same group for about two hours per day.

In addition to teaching the intensive class, we co-taught about one hundred undergraduate medical students every week for two hours to give them listening practice and an introduction to North American culture. They were packed together in one tiered lecture hall. Describing U.S. holidays with crudely drawn visuals was a mainstay at first. An evergreen tree to talk about Christmas. A turkey to talk about Thanksgiving. We usually had a structured activity and after that, we would ad lib slowly and distinctly in English about North American culture. As time went on, we got a bit more sophisticated in our topics. For instance, I talked about U.S. geography, and Fran talked about the American family.

For our intensive English course, we set up with naive confidence a curriculum to cover four domains of English—reading, writing, speaking, and listening. I had majored in English and Fran had double-majored in English and history. Neither of us yet had master's degrees. Even though our supervisor, Teacher Lin, had a master's degree in linguistics, he gave us a great deal of freedom over the curriculum. Our textbooks were pirated books from the United States or England that we chose and that were fairly decent. We used one for conversation that had current issues to discuss, such as air and water pollution. Another one had selected readings that made for lively discussions about such topics as women's rights in the Middle East or volunteerism in America.

In our first class, almost all of our students were in their 20s, just like us. The twenty-seven doctors and medical teachers had been selected out of two hundred who wanted to study English with us. In addition to learning the language during class time, they were expected to study for twenty hours or so each week on their own. It was a full-time proposition for them to study English and for us to keep up with them; they were friendly, eager, and diligent.

Fran, coming from teaching junior high in Boston, where there were regular fights in the classroom, had to pinch herself sometimes to make sure the new teaching setup was real. We were amazed that students were always in class early, made tea for us and kept it hot all class period, crowded around us at break, stayed an hour late after class, and wanted extra assignments. They even wanted to visit us on the weekends.

When the *waiban* started planning field trips that involved students, which we much preferred over being escorted to places by school officials, students took notebooks and said they wanted to "grasp the chance" to learn new, on-the-spot vocabulary. And if no notebook was handy, writing on one's hand would do. We wondered: how could these students be more ideal?

Students made a huge commitment to join our classes. We later learned they had signed contracts to say they would work the next ten years for Luzhou Medical College if they were selected to study with us! We observed that our students were participating in a new mass movement in China—a push to learn English—and were doing it with a fervor, passion, and diligence that we had never anticipated.

The students had already studied English for five or six years in junior high and high school; most had reached at least an intermediate level. A couple of cadres from the school took turns sitting at the back of the classroom, but they didn't interfere with anything. Cadres were people in positions of authority who were dedicated to the goals of the Communist Party. We didn't think they understood English, and we ignored them.

One thing that we both had to get used to was different cultural expectations in regard to personal space. Once Fran was showing students something on a wall map, only to turn around and find everyone right up in her face. Another thing we had to get used to was the periodic expression "*neige*," which we realized was like our expression "um" or "you know." Students so often inserted it in the middle of their sentences when they were speaking English that we took to fining students a few cents for each *neige* they uttered. The money was put in a kitty that we then used for the end-of-the-semester class party. Years later, we look back on this approach with chagrin. We were misguided to perceive languages as separate silos. They develop in an integrated way and, therefore, it was natural for sounds from Chinese to emerge as our students were developing English.

I'd had one methods course in how to teach English to speakers of other languages, but my only formal teaching experience had been to teach composition the previous semester at Sichuan Normal University in Chengdu. Despite the enthusiastic welcome from students, I harbored feelings of insecurity. I knew that students could turn on foreign teachers. I'd seen that happen with a Canadian colleague in Chengdu, who ended up teaching a group of unruly seniors. She found out they likely had been assigned to her because some of the Chinese teachers refused to teach them. I wrote in a March 6, 1986, journal entry about the Luzhou situation:

> I anticipate that we will have some cross-cultural crises after the students realize what a psychological, cross-cultural experience learning English intensively is. Perhaps they will skip classes or

refuse to do assignments or merely listen without response in class
. . . After they realize we are young, inexperienced teachers who
make mistakes, there will have to be a new acceptance and new
ground rules about the way we will teach and learn.

As time went by, Fran and I discovered that we had different teaching
styles. Fran was patient and taught everything step-by-step. Sometimes she
critiqued herself on her teaching skills, wishing she could simplify class
explanations. For example, she mourned the difficulty of teaching topic
sentences, feeling that the students were quite lost, partly because the sentences required a more linear organizational structure than they were used
to.

I tended to fly through material without frequently checking for understanding. I started out using old copies of *National Geographic* as a reading text for one class. The students spent eight hours of class time reading
one article. It took me a while to realize that the vocabulary was too hard
for the students and that reading *National Geographic* was not a good use
of class time.

Every day after class, the same group of about a half dozen students
would hang around until we were ready to leave the classroom, and then
they would escort us across campus to our rooms. They had been instructed
about what to do and what not to do in their interactions with us, and they
didn't expect to or ask to enter our apartment when we arrived at our door.
We walked as slowly as possible.

The students would rapidly fire random questions without trying to
follow the line of thought of the question another student had asked previously—like reporters calling out questions to a public figure.

"Miss Zehr, ought I to say 'I go there' or 'I go to there'?"
"Miss Zehr, have you been to Zigong? The Lantern Festival
there is beautiful."
"Miss Martens, do American parents really love their children,
or do they care only about money?"
"Miss Martens, do Americans really respect their old people?"
"Miss Martens, do Americans really volunteer to help other
people without getting paid for it?"
"Miss Zehr, what do you do with your spare time?"
"Miss Zehr, do you drink wine?"

As we quickly bonded with the students in our intensive English class,
we kept experimenting with activities we could do with them outside of

class that wouldn't be shut down by the *waiban*. Volleyball on an outside court, as well as ping-pong, was tolerated. Once we and our students played against the college's women's volleyball team and won. Generally, all outside activities on campus with people were acceptable, as long as it wasn't just with one person. If it only didn't rain so much in Luzhou!

꿎

On one occasion, when we were invited to attend a Teacher's Day celebration, we realized the extent to which students in China revered their teachers. In fact, much of this reverence clearly came from the country's strong Confucian roots; everyone was conscious of a hierarchy of authority and the duty of those lower on the scale to respect and honor those above them.

For this special day, teachers were honored with presents. We got silk fabric that we had picked out ourselves. There were long speeches—lasting two and a half hours—but there were some interesting stories and reflections from teachers, some having to do with exhortations to be kind and patient with students who were still disturbed by past historical events. There was an overall emphasis on helping students uphold Marxist principles—especially that of serving and helping others. Other reflections had to do with teachers watching over students' lives and even opposing inappropriate male–female relationships—in effect, to act like surrogate parents! We observed that teachers had leeway to deal with the private lives of students who seemed to be more dependent on parents and authority figures than typical U.S. college students.

The meeting also seemed to demonstrate to the new Chinese teachers the nobility and dignity of the profession of teaching. Teaching love of one's profession was clearly important in China, perhaps, we speculated, because many students did not get to choose their profession and needed to be taught to love it.

7

A Pragmatic Minder

Mary Ann

While we went about our daily routines, Teacher Luo was an ever-constant presence. The college *waiban* had assigned her to us as an "interpreter." A more accurate name for her role was "minder." It was her task to help us adjust and to monitor our activities. She lived in an apartment in the building across from us with some of the medical teachers who were our students. But at night, she slept in the tearoom underneath our bedrooms.

"I need to sleep here in case you have questions about something," Teacher Luo explained.

Teacher Luo spoke English fluently and was a kind and practical minder. She did not ask us personal questions. She didn't make small talk. She approached her assignment as a duty. She had that conscientious air of ardent Communist Party members. Her duty to serve her country in the moment meant paying attention to our activities and affairs. She seemed to have little curiosity about our personal lives or life in the United States.

For our first couple of weeks in Luzhou, Teacher Luo was usually around if we weren't in class. She ate lunch and dinner with us in our separate room in the dining hall so she could communicate our preferences regarding food to the cook. The cook or his helper brought in the plates of steaming *mapo doufu* (a wonderful combination of pork, tofu, peanuts, and spicy sauce) and bowls of rice or the final course of vegetables in broth. However, the cook could see for himself what we were leaving on the serving plates. He didn't need instructions from Teacher Luo to deduce that we were not touching the pickled vegetables that were a side dish to the usual rice gruel for breakfast. He eventually also deduced that we loved hot pot and his crackling rice dish, one that made loud popping noises.

We wondered how long it would take for us to grow weary of the constant scrutiny by Teacher Luo. At the same time, if the *waiban* required someone to watch our every move, we were grateful that it was Teacher Luo, because she was quietly present, not intrusive.

One morning at breakfast, Fran told me she thought she had heard a creature moving in her room in the night. She'd heard the plastic cover on a package of sugar cookies crackle, but when she'd gotten out of bed and shone a flashlight on the package, nothing looked suspicious.

In the afternoon, I heard a shriek and Fran calling out to me, "Come quick!" A rat was crouched on Fran's desk, chomping on an apple. Fran said she would watch the rat while I sought help. I ran out into the courtyard. On a balcony to the apartment building across from us, Teacher Luo was stretching her arms after waking from an afternoon nap.

"Uh. We have a slight problem," I said. "There's a rat on Fran's desk. Maybe you have an idea of how to get rid of it?"

By the time Teacher Luo and I got back to Fran's room, the rat had scampered under the bed and Fran was agitated. Teacher Luo thumped the suitcases under the bed to chase the rat out. Fran and I both squealed as we saw the rat pop its head out of the corner of a suitcase that contained Fran's clothes. Teacher Luo, grinning, zipped the suitcase shut, trapping the creature, and dragged the suitcase out onto the balcony outside Fran's room.

With quiet efficiency, Teacher Luo unzipped the suitcase at one corner and made a little hole for the rat to escape. Then she beat on the suitcase. The rat jumped out onto the balcony and then, to our amazement, leaped off it to the courtyard twenty feet below. The rat, demonstrating its invincibility, then ran the length of a gutter and disappeared. Teacher Luo was amused by our fear of rats. "If a rat comes into my room, I just catch it and kill it," she said. But she responded to our fear kindly. She immediately found a workman to nail a strip of plywood under each of our doors to seal them off from the outdoors.

For weeks we imagined we heard rats in the night. We'd think that perhaps we'd left a door open and a rat had slipped into our bedrooms. Though we each had our own room, one night we slept in the same bed because one of us had thought a rat was in her room. As the only two foreigners in

Luzhou, we needed to support each other. That time it was a false alarm. But in a strange country, it was easy to let our fears about rats get out of hand.

In addition to asking Teacher Luo to escort us to the post office several times a week so we could have a change in scenery, we tried to get her support to let us interact more with people. We told her we had heard from the director of our organization that Luzhou had a church, and we wanted to visit it. That was new information to her, she said, that the city had a church. But she relayed our message to the *waiban*, and the leaders replied they'd have to check if it was "open."

In early April, we received our first visitors to Luzhou: Ann Martin and Dale Taylor, who were English teachers with CEE in Chongqing. They had traveled eight hours by bus on a Friday to spend the weekend with us. Fran and I introduced our expatriate friends to our intensive English students. We were so proud of how much English they had learned in our classes in six weeks. Fran and I had bought oranges, candy, and tea and had worked with our students to set up the classroom for a party, in accordance with the customs in China. Our students were wonderful—they made colorful chalk drawings on the blackboard and heated up water for tea.

After we welcomed everyone, the students introduced themselves and gave short welcome speeches. Then Ann, who is American, and Dale, who is Canadian, talked about themselves. After that, questions were fair game:

> "What will you buy in China to take home?"
> "Are there mountains in Canada?"
> "What is an American folk tale?"
> "What is the education system in Canada like?"
> "Do writers make money in the United States?"

I'm sure that Fran and I made mistakes opening and closing the party. But our students ate all the snacks, which was a sign they were at ease.

Back in our rooms, we four foreign teachers relaxed and talked about our families, future plans, and books we were reading; we also made observations about the intriguing country in which we lived. We noticed that Teacher Luo was off duty while we received our visitors in our rooms. It was not part of her responsibility to monitor our interactions with other foreigners. We suspected that must have been a great relief to her.

8

The Celebrity Life

FRAN

ONE DAY IN LUZHOU, when we were once again being treated as the center of an event, I turned to Mary Ann and said, "So this is what it feels like to be a celebrity. What do you think?"

In fact, we thought a variety of things. There was a certain thrill to being known to nearly every person in town; everyone knew us even though we knew few of them. They knew us from our walks through town. Every time we stopped and bought something, like paper and pens, cassette tapes, or cans of food, or bargained in the market for something, usually tangerines and vegetables, a crowd formed and the question hung in the air: What will the foreigners, the *waiguoren*, do today? Children giggled and ran from us; young men would shout "Hello!" from across the street. One man, startled to see us and turning his head to look, crashed his bicycle. While at the market one day, I overheard two elderly Chinese women talking about us. My Chinese was good enough by that point to catch what they were saying.

"Where do you think they are from? Russia maybe?"

"I do not know. I think, well, I am guessing they are from Japan."

Japan?! I thought, smiling inwardly.

Almost everywhere we went, we created a stir. And after a while, it got exhausting. We hesitated about going out, asking ourselves if we were really up to the attention that day. We began to sympathize with Hollywood celebrities who have to be on constant alert for the paparazzi every time they step out their front door. We saw the point of low-slung hats and dark glasses—although those would not help us, since our foreignness revealed itself in every stitch of clothing, every step we took, every time we opened our mouths. We could not escape attention.

In addition to townspeople seeing us in person on a regular basis, they saw us on TV. We once counted up the times we had been on local TV: seven.

There was the time Mary Ann was filmed in a commercial for the kind of umbrella—oiled paper on a bamboo frame—that Luzhou is famous for. I was in class, so Mary Ann accepted brightly colored parasols for the "foreign friends." She shook the hand of the umbrella factory manager and then opened and closed an umbrella for the camera with an expression of absolute admiration.

Then there was the time we were ferried out to a large boat on the Yangtze River in order to have the best view of the dragon boat races, held for the first time in Luzhou since the Cultural Revolution. In this case, Luzhou was one year behind the changing times; other cities had resumed the tradition the year before. We joined the Luzhou mayor, a few overseas Chinese people, and some bureaucrats on the boat. We were filmed as each boat—red, yellow, green, blue—with a dragon head on the stern was rowed up to our big one, where, from our deck on high, we practiced our celebrity waves, beaming down on the full crew at the oars. In addition to the twenty or so oarsmen, each boat had a drummer, cymbals clanger, and flag man to keep up a rhythm. It felt like when the queen and king blessed the knightly jousters of old astride their splendid steeds. As far as we could see in all directions, people cheered their favorite teams from balconies and roofs and the shores of the Yangtze.

Another time, when our CEE leaders came, we were on TV for half an hour, walking around the college campus with forced smiles, viewing X-ray machines and acupuncture rooms where doctors were sticking needles in someone's head and twisting them, trying to cure partial paralysis resulting from cerebral bleeding.

One Saturday, the school leaders invited us to a basketball game. The game was being played in town, and we would have preferred to walk. But in the usual style of treating us as dignitaries, the leaders arranged for a car—a Russian Volga—and a driver for us. Mary Ann could smell gas fumes in the car, and they didn't agree with her stomach.

Teams compete in dragon boat races on the Yangtze River.

When we arrived, we were seated prominently behind a tea table in the stands above the center line of a basketball court of the outdoor stadium to watch the game. Filming of the players, which regularly panned to us as "entranced spectators," was well underway when Mary Ann turned to me with a pale face and said, "I don't feel well. I think I am going to be sick." I hurriedly turned to our official escorts to try to explain the problem. In the meantime, Mary Ann stood up to try to find a restroom. Unfortunately, she didn't get very far. All of a sudden, she vomited in the stands and also in front of the camera. After some moments of confusion and dismay on the part of all those affected, Mary Ann was hustled away. Anxious to get out of the limelight as well, I hurried after them, hoping that the disturbing interruption would be edited out before it aired that night. For weeks, random people came up to Mary Ann and asked if she was feeling better.

We also made our appearance on TV for various other events, such as a student military marching demonstration at the school track on Independence Day and formal visits to lychee and longan orchards. We were often uncomfortable with our status as *waiguoren* (people from the outside) or *da bizi* (big noses) or the term that sometimes young children used, *yang-guizi* (foreign devils or ghosts). It was hard to fit in. We were always the outsiders, and we realized that even if we were in China for twenty or thirty years, we would always be seen as outsiders—even if that meant we were sometimes put up on a pedestal or treated with deference.

There was at least one place in Luzhou, however, where we were not singled out and given preferential treatment: the post office. When we entered the building, there was usually a chaotic scene in front of the long counter. Many people were jostling to pick up packages or mail letters; there was no orderly queue. The practice, we noticed, was to hold paper currency and wave it to get someone behind the counter to pay attention, so we adopted that strategy. The workers did not seem to be in a particular hurry to help us. We tried to zero in on postal workers who had kind faces, but we usually had a fairly lengthy stay at the postal office and became reconciled to that.

As time went on, I noticed a dimming of the spotlight, much less fuss about these exotic teachers from a land far, far away. There were fewer TV appearances, fewer banquets, fewer field trips with the authorities— in short, a much-improved life for us *waiguoren*. We could act like more "normal" people again. However, I must acknowledge that we would not have fared well living as our students did, which would have meant living with four other people in a single room, walking to a common bathhouse to bathe, doing without a washing machine and electric heater (thus getting chilblains on our fingers and toes like our students did), and making routine phone calls from a downtown post office. As with most things, we sought a balance—and that balance, as with many things in China, was often elusive.

9

Stories and Folk Songs in the Stone Forest

Mary Ann

A visit to Xingwen Stone Forest with our first intensive English class

TEACHER LIN, A WIRY and quick-moving man with an angular face, was the number-two person in the *waiban*. He seemed to have the power to make a big difference in our quality of life, materially and socially. The 40-something Teacher Lin initially also really wowed us with his lively personality, excellent command of English, and understanding of American culture. It was evident he had been alert and engaged during the two years he'd lived and studied at Ohio State University.

Teacher Lin made arrangements for us to interact with groups in Luzhou, and he accompanied us to these events. One spring weekend, for example, he arranged for us to speak with some local high school English teachers. Fran and I talked a little about ourselves and then invited questions. Most of the questions were based on stereotypes Chinese people had about U.S. society. The teachers asked about race relations, material goods, volunteering, the standard of living, and crime.

Teacher Lin told us afterward that when he was asked to speak to similar groups in the United States, Americans would ask: "Do women in China still bind their feet?" (China had outlawed foot-binding in 1912.) Teacher Lin was making the point that both Americans and Chinese people could be grossly uninformed.

During our first semester, Teacher Lin rolled out the red carpet for us by giving us material comforts. I think he soon realized that we considered our accommodations to be very comfortable, but what we felt was missing was social interaction. Teacher Lin was someone who toed the Communist Party line, which meant he felt responsible for limiting our influence. He also wanted us to be happy so that we would stay at the college. In that spirit, in May, three months after our arrival, he planned an overnight field trip for us and all the students in our intensive English class. Except for the fact that Teacher Lin arranged for Fran and me to sit with him at a separate table for meals instead of sitting with our students, who talked and laughed loudly as they drank beer and ate, we were delighted with all the arrangements and with how the trip went off.

The trip was to the Xingwen Stone Forest, near the town of Yibin, a four-hour trip by bus from Luzhou. The area was remote. We bumped over a terrible road to get there. On the way we saw vast rice paddies and fields of wheat and corn. Chinese farmers use every possible plot of arable land for growing crops. We saw worker brigades transplanting rice seedlings in the hot sun. We spotted junks, which people lived in, on a river. Later, I wrote haikus based on my impressions of China's countryside:

> Straw hats hide faces
> of farmers planting rice
> seedlings, one by one.

Bamboo rustles
and kowtows to clay roof tiles,
announcing a storm.

The students all spoke in English on the trip, even with each other. We hadn't told them to do so, but they apparently interpreted the field trip to be an extended English conversation, or maybe they had been instructed by Teacher Lin to speak English.

When we arrived, we first visited a cave, which had well-laid stone steps inside it and colored lights next to particularly beautiful formations, but very few visitors. The largest room was one hundred meters high, with an opening in the ceiling where sunlight streamed through and enveloped a tiny stream of water trickling down into the cave. According to a tour guide that our students consulted, visitors had imagined the cave formations to be people or legendary creatures. We saw formations that looked like a woman serving guests a cup of tea, a dragon spine, a dove, a monk, a group of monkeys, a peach, a hot pepper, a wall of flowers, and a lake of fairies.

That evening we walked in the countryside. Some of the students started sharing stories from their past about working in the countryside during the Cultural Revolution, because the surroundings reminded them of it. These were students who had been born in 1957 and 1958, and they were nearly 30 years old when we taught them. Most of the students in our class had been born between 1960 and 1965 and were young enough to have avoided being assigned to live in the countryside. It had also been possible, our students said, to escape being sent to a rural area if one had parents with political power or a job in a big city. During the Cultural Revolution, students could gain entrance to college if they had connections. The colleges filled up with the proletariat—workers and peasants. Schools did not have admissions testing until the end of the Cultural Revolution in 1976.

One student said that during the Cultural Revolution, he had labored in the same county that we were now visiting. He had planted and processed green tea, rice, and wheat. Another student had spent several years planting rice and corn.

৩৫৬

A prominent storyteller in the stone forest was Hu Bing, one of our most independent-thinking and intellectually curious students. He was a natural leader with earnest eyes and a charismatic manner. He was the same student who had been the first to invite us to his home and then had needed to rescind the invitation.

Hu Bing took every opportunity to get to know more about the world outside of China through us. Yet he never treated us as anything loftier than what we were—two ordinary women in their 20s.

"When I was sent out to the countryside, to stimulate my mind, I read a dictionary," Hu Bing said, smiling. It had been his job to "introduce wheat."

"We had to report to Chairman Mao three times a day," another student added. "We bowed to a picture of Chairman Mao on the wall and recited words from him."

A student stood up and did a little fast-paced dance to show how children danced in praise of Chairman Mao. Everyone laughed, so we did too.

Late in the evening the students sang Chinese folk songs or international folk songs—Russian, Yugoslavian, Japanese, and American. Teacher Lin, who had uncharacteristically shed his jacket during our activities, played the harmonica. About that night Fran wrote:

> I could really feel absorbed into the culture. Beautiful traditions and a sense of history. They [students] complain sometimes of the shackles of the feudal system, but it seems it is still valuable on one level. Honestly, the young people are SO impatient sometimes because they're not "developed" and they want China to hurry, hurry and get with it! It's surprising sometimes to hear the criticism of the systems—somebody even mentioned that Communism keeps the exceptional from fully using their talents because then they would be set apart from others and all are to be equal in society. So, it becomes a good theory but loses something in practice. . . . But morality is high here in some aspects—particularly in strict sexual standards, crime, and the value placed on honesty—the most prized value.

The next day we hiked for several hours looking for interesting formations in the stone forest: the seven fairies, the husband and wife (two tall stones standing side by side), the mushroom stone, and the meadow of sheep. We saw a funnel valley that the students told us was a world geological wonder.

We were a smartly dressed group as we plodded along a path through corn plant stubble, trying to spot and match formations with the descriptions in a guide for tourists. The men wore tailored casual jackets and jeans. The women wore dresses with brightly colored solid fabrics, which would have been considered bourgeois only several years previously. Zhang Dongni, a student who we could not have anticipated would soon be assigned to be our interpreter, wore bright red. Another student wore a sage-green dress, trimmed with a ruffle, and yet another wore a wine-colored dress and donned a straw hat. Teacher Lin had a camera. So did Fran and I. Our students didn't own cameras. We took a lot of photos of them.

Although stone formations are a popular Chinese tourist attraction, we didn't meet other tourists. We rambled in the rocky, rolling countryside for a whole morning before heading back to Luzhou.

The outing offered a good chance for our students to improve their English fluency. Teacher Lin complimented all of us because the students were quickly gaining conversational fluency in English. He had taught many of them previously and had helped them to gain a good foundation in English.

The field trip to the stone forest gave Fran and me the kind of social interaction with Chinese young people that we craved, and it boosted our mental health. Teacher Lin had made a special trip—traveling for about eight hours round trip—before our class visit so that he could scope out the setting and arrange for our lodging and meals. Sichuan had telephones, but people didn't seem to use them much.

Teacher Lin kept a close watch on Fran and me. At the same time, by planning the overnight outing, Teacher Lin had been a facilitator of friendship.

Our glamorous students in the stone forest

10

The Disco Teachers

FRAN

AT TIMES, VERY ODD things happened in the course of our teaching. Mary Ann and I were occasionally asked to give campus-wide lectures about American culture and American holidays. For one such lecture, the college advertised the event by putting up posters around campus. If anyone were to tell us that we had advertised ourselves on a poster, scantily clad in bikini-like outfits and posing with lecture pointers in a stance akin to a Travolta disco freeze, we would have said they were daft. But, on the other hand, this surely wasn't the first time in China that things concerning us had been totally out of our hands,

The odd incident regarding the poster occurred when Luzhou Medical College was hosting Atlee and Winifred Beechy for two days. They were an elderly, staid, and benevolent Mennonite couple sent from the United States to China by CEE to check in on how Fran and I—and other CEE teachers—were faring in our posts.

During their visit, the Beechys met me after class with smirks on their faces. "Some poster they have of you two hanging up on campus!" When pushed for details, they only urged us to look, which we did. But we saw only a simple poster with bold, black letters proclaiming the upcoming event, with a sea of upturned audience faces painted in below.

We remained mystified until later, when one of our students gave us the "whole picture." She came up to me and declared, "I thought you said that film *Mr. No Legs* was an unrealistic picture of American life." I nodded, thinking of the low-budget flick we had barely stomached the week before. It seemed to Mary Ann and me that our college intentionally found unsavory B- or C-rated films to impress upon its young students how depraved Western culture was. "And you said that the woman who always walked around with little clothing wasn't like ordinary women in the U.S?" Again, I agreed. "Then why did you give permission to show yourselves like that woman on the poster near the sportsground?"

I spluttered, "What? No, you please explain to *us*." She explained that the teaching department head had okayed an artist's portrayal of the foreign teachers prancing around stage lecturing (or was it discoing?) in less-than-modest costumes.

Soon after it was posted, some students, knowing our respectable characters, decided to take it down; one student took it home and put it in his wife's hands for safekeeping. The teaching department head discovered it missing, tracked down the thief, and restored the poster to its original place.

Next, enter the Beechys, whose excessive interest in the picture (they wanted to take a snapshot of it) worried the college leaders accompanying them. Could it be that something was wrong with this portrayal of the American character? Later, an emergency discussion was held, and the teaching department head, under fire, cleverly saved face by passing the buck. "Yes," he said, "the foreign teachers have seen and approved the poster. So I put it up." Nonetheless, the verdict was to cut off the offending part, and that was the condition it was in when we first saw it.

It was a lot of fuss over a picture we never laid eyes on. It's too bad we never saw it, though. Not that it really matters but, well, some things are best not left to the imagination!

ॐ

Not long after the "disco" lecture, we were whisked away by the *waiban* to a "special show" that they were excited to show us. We witnessed how China was trying to bring in something of the Western culture to attract the young people. We went to a variety show downtown that mixed traditional folk songs with disco numbers and comedy acts. Disco lights, multicolored, swept over the audience. Songs with a monotonous dance beat played on an electronic keyboard. It was hard to get our heads around the disparate elements. The audience, which included middle-aged people, clapped loudest for the folk songs.

11

Taiji and Longing

Mary Ann

In parks, elderly people practiced the daily exercise routine of *taijiquan*, a kind of martial art, in the early daylight hours. They looked so graceful, partly crouching and moving their arms like ballet dancers in slow motion. Morning fog often enveloped the *taiji* exercisers, creating an ethereal aura. Fran suggested that we should learn *taiji* as a way to connect with Chinese culture and get out of our apartment to interact with people. I was skeptical that I could learn it, but I didn't want to dismiss her idea, and in Luzhou, if we didn't do it together, it wouldn't be feasible for her to do it at all, so I was willing.

A physical education teacher consented to teach us *taiji* because he was motivated to practice English. Wang Kai was a fit and tall man in his 20s. He met us for ninety minutes after dark a couple of times a week in a tracksuit on the basketball court. Fran and I wore sweatpants and T-shirts. The lessons were an "unofficial activity"—not initiated by the *waiban*—so it seemed best to meet at night to reduce the chance of anyone finding out about the lessons and canceling them. Plus, we didn't want spectators.

Wang Kai was dedicated, strict, and kind. He had a solemnity about him. As we learned each move, he had us redo the routine each time from the beginning. If we made a mistake with the newest move, we had to start the routine all over again. He used short English commands. He taught us the poetic names of the moves, such as "grasping the peacock's tail." But mostly Wang Kai demonstrated the moves, and we tried to imitate him.

47

Fran was more coordinated than I was, and the routine came easier to her. I felt awkward and a bit silly in making the deliberate, slow-motion moves.

Wang Kai wasn't chatty, but one time he shared that he was frustrated about a lack of "freedom." He said he had been offered a position to coach basketball in Chengdu, but he hadn't been allowed by the college leaders to accept the position. This was a typical problem stemming from rigid job assignments in China.

After studying for two months with Wang Kai, we had learned the whole routine. According to our teacher, it had taken us only four times as long as it usually took a whole class of his students to learn it. We didn't think that was too bad, given that the form of exercise was new to us as foreigners. Of course, we had internalized the beginning of the routine far better than the end of it because we were constantly restarting it. We planned to continue the lessons so we could improve the routine. Wang Kai complimented us, saying, "You have mastered it, but you still make some small mistakes."

Wang Kai was not one of our English students, so we didn't spend time with him outside of our *taiji* lessons. He lived in the apartment building across from us, and occasionally we would pass him as he went to the dining hall and we returned from the dining hall where we ate our meals. *Ni chi fan le ma* ("Have you eaten?"), we'd ask each other. *Chi le* ("I've eaten"), or *Meiyou chi* ("I haven't eaten"), was the polite response.

One day when Fran was outside of the apartment alone, Wang Kai handed her a letter. To our surprise, Wang Kai had written a love letter to me. It was customary in Chinese culture that he would give the letter to an intermediary—a friend—rather than to me directly. It was handwritten in English on semitransparent rice paper and slipped into an envelope with a willowy female figure on it. He wrote:

> Dear Miss Zehr:
>
> Being a chinese man, I really don't know how to express my feeling for you. Ever since I had met you, especially since the day I had been invited as your coach, I have been miserable. Never before I met a girl like you, from a country I know little, behave differently, so strange and mysteries, so frank and tender. I am drunk with air of your noble. I am longing to see you all the time, but I dare not to see you. When I meet you, I am not myself. I fear to meet you and talk with you, because I know it's a hopeless. For several times, I had avoided to meet you when I saw you and Miss Mardons [Martens] walking in the campus. It's not polite, but I

could only do so. Now, as the time going on, I really cannot bear it. Though it's sound ridiculous in such a small town in Luzhou. Though others may laugh at me. Some people may get hot about the action. I must let you know my heart.

We chinese people are often embarrassed to show their affection to a young girl. Surely I am yet to do. I don't know how you think of me, but I believe you are surely to treat the matter properly.

Eagerly for an answer from you,
your devoted Wang

I hadn't known that Wang Kai knew so much English. Maybe he didn't, and someone else had written the letter for him. I found it ironic that while I was feeling like a clunky, uncoordinated person during the *taiji* lessons, Wang Kai had apparently developed a positive impression of me. I found particularly moving his observation of how I behaved differently than women he knew, "so strange and mysteries, so frank and tender." The part about his being "drunk" with my "noble" was over the top. Wang Kai certainly gave Fran and me something to talk about for a few days. Because of the political climate, I didn't consider dating Chinese men, though I was attracted to some. For example, back in Chengdu, I'd accepted the invitation of a student in my young teachers' class to tour Chengdu for a day, and we'd had a great time riding bikes around the city, visiting a temple, and having tea together. It was not a date but rather a chance for him to practice English; he had a girlfriend. It hadn't escaped me, though, that he was well-dressed in a turtleneck, a tan tailored blazer, and slim-legged gray slacks, and that he was very handsome. I took a photo of him posing confidently in front of the temple, deliberately smiling only slightly, and he took a photo of me grinning and holding a cup of tea to my lips in a teahouse.

I had not thought about Wang Kai in a romantic way. I was touched that he had reached out to me and written such beautiful words. I also recognized that as a foreigner, I represented a life outside of Luzhou and China, and the affection he expressed for me might have had more to do with the fact that I was American than anything else. His profession of his attraction to me might have been entangled with a dream to leave Luzhou. Everyone knew that Fran had a boyfriend living abroad, and I didn't. Therefore, I got the letter.

If I wanted to keep my job, it was out of the question to even walk alone with a man my age, let alone date anyone in Luzhou. Teacher Lin and the other officials in the *waiban* once visited Fran and me in our tearoom to officially inform us we couldn't date Chinese men. They solemnly read to us a decree that said we were forbidden to have any romantic relationships— or sex—with Chinese people. Soon after I left Luzhou, the officials handed Fran an "important notice for American citizens" elaborating on "illicit relations with Chinese nationals." It was typed on the letterhead of the U.S. Consulate General and cautioned that Chinese authorities consider it to be "a violation of regulations" for foreigners to "entertain" Chinese guests in a hotel or dormitory. It also reported that some foreigners had been detained, questioned, and "heavily fined" by Chinese police because of "relationships with Chinese nationals of the opposite sex."[1] Was the memo issued by recommendation of Chinese authorities, or had the consulate general initiated the memo on its own accord? One motivation for Chinese authorities to prohibit sexual relationships between foreigners and Chinese people was that Chinese government leaders had heard reports of AIDS in the West, and they didn't want the disease to spread to China. In fact, in the fall of 1987, Fran and other foreign teachers were forced to take tests to prove they didn't have AIDS.

৩৻৶

Fran and I were in shock that Wang Kai had been so bold as to write a foreigner a love letter. Wang Kai did acknowledge that "some people may get hot about the action." But how was it that he could be so careless about the possible repercussions if the *waiban* learned he had written the letter? Fran and I were concerned that Wang Kai would get into trouble that could affect his job opportunities if word got out about what he had done. We felt protective of him.

I'd noticed an earnestness about Wang Kai when he taught us *taiji*. He didn't seem to be the kind of person to make things up. Therefore, I took his words at face value. I wrote a letter back to him. I told him that I was honored by his lovely words and devotion. However, we would not be able to pursue a romance. It was forbidden in the current political climate.

Fran delivered my letter to him and told him it would be best if we discontinued the *taiji* lessons. It was a loss because we had enjoyed them. We didn't tell a soul about the incident.

---

1. Consulate General of the United States of America, "Important Notice."

What made me sad was that Wang Kai avoided me after he got my response. We never passed him again while walking back from our meals to our apartment. I imagine that he watched for when we left our apartment so that he could go out to the dining hall to get his meal at a different time. It pained me to think of the burden of his deliberately planning on a daily basis *not* to casually run into me.

I have kept his letter all these years. It's a symbol to me that a totalitarian society can never completely control a person's feelings or actions. Wang Kai had been undeterred.

12

Our Spunky Interpreter

FRAN

OUR STERN, ALOOF, AND oft-knitting translator, Teacher Luo, relinquished her post after our first semester. We surmised that she was relieved not to have to traipse down to the post office with us once or twice a week. Mary Ann and I were fortunate to gain a new translator, Zhang Dongni, who became our dearest friend and confidant in Luzhou. She had long black hair, glasses, an open countenance, inquiring eyes, and an infectious laugh. Also, she was much younger than Teacher Luo, a student, and a daughter of one of the medical faculty on campus. When she first came to us, she spoke halting English even though she had been in our intensive English class during our first semester. Since our Chinese was progressing at a crawl, we had much work to communicate with each other. Sometimes, in the middle of translating, Zhang would burst into a giggling fit, and then it was even harder to understand a word. She called me "France" or "Frans." She was like a burst of sunlight in an otherwise often cloudy environment, both literally and figuratively.

We felt that Zhang Dongni was an essential link to the society around us. She worked as a secretary for the *waiban* and relayed messages to us. She was also our guard, sleeping in the tearoom on the floor below us, as had Teacher Luo. However, she did not seem to have qualms about telling us some of the local stories and gossip, and she seemed to have a way of persuading the leaders to let us attend some events that perhaps had been ruled out previously.

Unlike many of the people we met on campus, Zhang was unguarded in her remarks and quite open about her opinions. "What do you think?" was her frequent question to us, as we all tried to navigate the complex and restrictive world of Luzhou Medical College. She often provided us with a behind-the-scenes look at what was happening in meetings and decisions about us, though equally as often she was left in the dark and was guessing alongside us. The *waiban* might have expected Zhang to play the role of minder, but that simply didn't work for someone with such a trusting personality. She slept a few nights in the room under ours as part of her job, but she soon abandoned this practice and slept at home in her own bed.

Unlike Teacher Luo, Zhang was curious about our American culture and willing to join in on our cultural celebrations. Once we filled up a bucket of water, and Zhang joined us in our strange cultural practice of bobbing for apples to mark the holiday of Halloween.

Even after she was no longer our student, Zhang often sat at the back of our classroom and took notes, subsequently giving us good tips about teaching. She also occasionally gave us glimpses into Chinese culture. One time she mentioned that for her and other students, it was important not to stand out too much. A person who was too different or opinionated would be pushed back down to join the rest, like in a whack-a-mole game—but this was no game.

Zhang loved to talk with us about matters of the heart—love, boyfriends, marriage. She filled us in on which of our students were getting married and how courtship worked in Luzhou. She said that couples usually had a "go-between"—a peer or relative—who introduced them to each other. They would meet secretly somewhere for a short time to discern whether they wanted to be together, since dating was on the level of what Westerners would consider an engagement. We saw couples meeting in the shadows on campus after dark. To announce their decision to be a couple, they would go out into the streets on a Sunday, usually walking about a yard apart but in broad daylight. Breakups after the public appearance as a couple were rare. Most people married the first or second person they dated. One time, a couple scrawled "truly lovers" in Chinese in white chalk on a bench near our apartment; the surrounding camphor trees would have provided privacy. Mary Ann wrote a haiku based on what we learned about courting in Luzhou.

Self-conscious lovers
stroll on Sunday streets,
making couplehood public.

Zhang was curious about what kind of romantic relationship we felt was healthy and wondered how she could maintain her own identity within such a relationship. Mary Ann and I regularly spouted our deeply felt feminist views about egalitarian relationships and the importance of not relying on a man for one's happiness.

Because she knew I had a boyfriend, I was often the target of her inquiries about relationships. She wanted to know everything: how we had met, why we liked each other, how we dealt with disagreements, if we were planning to get married, and how we could maintain a long-distance relationship. On this last point, I did admit it was extremely difficult. We mainly communicated by writing long letters to each other (no email then). It was hard to be creative. Ken once sent me cookies he had made in a Dutch oven in his round hut rondavel. They were a crumbly mess when they arrived. He also once asked Mary Ann to buy flowers for me, but her search in the town for them turned up nothing. The distance between us, both physical and emotional, sometimes seemed too immense and vast to navigate.

Zhang also often brought up the topic of religion. At one point, she asked, "What does your religion have to offer that the Chinese people would need? I mean, we have a moral lifestyle and we manage fine on our own." After thinking this over, I remarked, "Yes, you are right. Well, perhaps the concept of forgiveness is needed. I have observed that people seem to often hold grudges against others."

Later that month, Zhang facilitated a party to make *jiaozi* (pork dumplings) with some of our students from the Luzhou Chemical Company. The five men obtained special permission from the college to come to our house to cook one Sunday. Two of them were middle-aged and three were young. We surmised that Luzhou Medical College received a hefty fee for their being in the intensive English class. Because the men were living in a simple dormitory, they had no equipment or supplies for cooking. With Zhang's help, they came up with most of what we needed: oil, flour, meat, vegetables, and salt. Zhang brought glasses from her house, and we borrowed bowls and chopsticks from the dining hall. Someone even swiped some hot pepper sauce from the dining hall. The men were extremely organized. Everyone was assigned a task and completed it well.

We found the conversation of our guests to be light and laced with humor. They also constructively advised us on our poor cooking skills, and we willingly submitted to a couple of hours of training. At the end, they said our skills were only so-so. It was not easy to make *jiaozi*, a process that reminded me a little of making the Russian dumplings, *verenika*, inherited from my Mennonite ancestors as a result of their sojourn in Russia.

Zhang Dongni was one of the few who successfully navigated a dinner invitation for us to visit her parents, who lived in an apartment on campus, a pleasant one nestled among the trees that grew profusely on the mountainside. We had a much better meal than we would have gotten in the dining hall, where food tended to be on the greasy side for our stomachs but was considered a sign of deference since oil used to be in short supply. The delicious meal consisted of roasted duck, hot seasoned beef, fungi and meat, a vegetable dish, sweet-and-sour fish, and celery-like soup. And before the meal we were offered oranges, sweets, and tea, as is the custom.

Zhang's parents had important positions in the college. Her father taught pathology, and her mother was a physician. During our meal, Zhang's father talked to us about his cancer research, alerting us to the danger of eating charred or overcooked food. No more of my favorite, burned toast, I thought.

Everyone enjoyed looking at our photo albums that we had brought along. They were surprised by the size of American homes and by any affection displayed in photographs. Zhang was thrilled to be able to invite us to her home; it was a warm and friendly evening together.

ᘺᘺ

On a day-to-day basis, Zhang told us a lot about Chinese and Luzhou life—many things she could have gotten in trouble for. In November 1986, Mary Ann wrote the following to her parents:

> You can forget about what I implied earlier, that restrictions seem a little less this term. On the way to lunch I just met Zhang Dongni who said that the leaders had found out about a cooking party we had arranged with a former student and his wife this weekend. (Actually, she innocently told them and they jumped on her for not knowing this was "impossible." They gave her some documents to read concerning dealings with foreigners and "criticized" her.) What happens in these cases is that the student is criticized and we

never know what happened; maybe the student cancels the event for another reason or just stops being friendly. You shouldn't think that this tight of a rein is true across China—the open cities are quite open. But definitely, Luzhou is conservative, conservative. I haven't heard stories like the ones we have to tell from anyone else living in China now. How can such kind leaders be so staunch!

Zhang showed her affection for us very openly. Walking across campus or while on field trips with the *waiban,* we had to get used to Zhang hanging onto us or intertwining her fingers with ours, a very common practice between two girls or two boys as they walked. The amount of physical touch surprised us, coming from what we perceived as a formal and dictatorial society.

It was such a relief to finally have a companion in Luzhou who seemed to have empathy for us and to see us as the humans we were when we were confused about cultural practices or some decision the *waiban* had made. We sensed Zhang was trying her best to fill us in, and that made us feel less paranoid and more at ease in Luzhou. And it was good for our mental health to interact daily with a warmhearted Chinese person our age who didn't take herself or us too seriously.

When my parents came to visit the college, Zhang was quite enamored of them. In a letter to my mother, Zhang wrote, "I will never forget those days when we were together. You have a strong and good impression on me. Your soft voice, kind heart, affable, amiable, especially your lecture and lesson and teaching conscientiously . . . I am determined to speak English. When they [Mary Ann and Fran] are at their home, we talk and do anything freely and easily as we like . . . we have a good time." Zhang also wrote about a National Day Party (October 1) that we had with students, for which we roped her into a play about the adventures of Tom Sawyer. Every time my mother sent a letter to me, Zhang would sit on my bed and make me explain its contents, always waiting patiently for the line "Say Hi to Zhang."

**Fran's parents, Elmer and Phyllis Martens,
with medical professionals at Luzhou Medical College**

13

Fran, Mary Ann, and Men

FRAN

"I FEEL LIKE A teaching machine!" I complained to Mary Ann after yet another meeting with the foreign affairs office. It was not just our thoughts and emotions that seemed to be disregarded by the college leaders; it was also our identity as women. In part because of the utilitarian focus on our skills and native English, we felt rather asexualized. We were actively discouraged from forming romantic relationships, both implicitly by our organization and explicitly by the Chinese authorities.

A while after we started our assignment, a young teacher in his 20s, Liu Yuling, came to Luzhou. Teacher Liu was tall and lanky with a narrow chin and intense dark eyes. He usually wore jeans, a sports jacket, and sneakers. Liu was from the crowded metropolitan city of Chongqing. Since he was used to the easy give-and-take of relationships with foreigners, the same type of environment Mary Ann had been familiar with in the city of Chengdu, it was not surprising that he immediately struck up a friendship with us.

Flattered by the attention of this handsome young man with conversant English, we took him up on the offer to stroll around town one Saturday. On the long walk down stone streets to the downtown area, Teacher Liu asked about the idea of starting a group Bible study with Luzhou colleagues. Surprised, we cautiously replied that we were not sure that would be allowed. Teacher Liu seemed taken aback but did not pursue the topic further.

The following weekend, Teacher Liu mentioned a film that was coming to the college cinema and asked if we wanted to go. Although we were not so keen on kung fu movies with all the fantastical flips in the air and slow-motion fighting, we agreed to go. We sat near the front of the theater, with Teacher Liu in the middle. We could not deny that it was pleasant to sit in a darkened theater with a young man who was whispering English translations of the dialogues in our ears, turning his head first to one side and then the other.

We emerged from the theater oblivious to the stares of other moviegoers and invited Teacher Liu to tea. Our conversation was wide-ranging; we were eager to hear his experiences and thoughts, and he was equally eager to hear ours. When he left, we looked at each other with bright eyes—it had been so long since we had received any male attention.

A few days later, Mary Ann and I were walking around the campus grounds when we spotted Teacher Liu. We waved and headed toward him. But there was an expression on his face that we could not read. Later, we decided the look was one of a whipped dog. He greeted us and then said he was busy and needed to go, turning abruptly and striding away. We were struck by the cold reception. What had happened? Had we offended him?

We later heard the truth from our interpreter, Zhang Dongni. "You know your friend, Teacher Liu?" she asked us breathlessly one afternoon. "He was—he had to go to a meeting. He had to tell a—what do you call it?— a self-confession. In front of all the college leaders. He can't meet with you anymore. It is not allowed." We were speechless. We did not know exactly what that meant—only that there was some heavy-handed psychological component. After Zhang gave us more details, we felt partly guilty and partly sad—both for him and for us. It looked like we were back to being teaching machines, and for Teacher Liu? We hoped there was no lasting damage; what a harsh way for him to be put in his place.

Given the paucity of easygoing male-female interaction, it was hardly surprising that on our travels, Mary Ann and I enjoyed the company of Western men we encountered at various tourist hot spots. Two Canadians caught our attention on a trip to the world-famous limestone mountains of Guilin in the winter of 1987.

Mary Ann and I met Richard and Dick on a boat we were taking down the shallow Li River. It was a twelve-fifteen seater filled with Germans, Brits, Soviets, and us. The weather was icy cold and misty; snatches of limestone mountains appeared somewhere above us.

We joked with the Canadians, giving names for odd-shaped peaks like "Melting Ice-Cream Mountain" instead of the official "Nine Horses Peak" or "The Three Mourning Widows." We watched, fascinated, as the cormorant fishermen on rickety boats sent their birds down into the water, each with a rope around its foot and a ring around its neck to prevent it from swallowing the fish it caught. Later, Mary Ann wrote a haiku about this sight:

> Silent fishermen
> Send feathered dolphins diving
> For silver fishes.

Women wash clothes in the Li River near Guilin.

The next day, the four of us decided to head to Guilin and the famous caves. Stepping into the largest cavern, we caught our breath. This was the most massive cavern we had ever seen. There were flights of steps built into the rock, and here and there shone garish, colored lights highlighting stalactites and stalagmites—all of which, again, had names: "The Three Gracious Sisters," "Flapping Elephant Ears," "Buffalo Head in Bamboo," and, of course, our own crazy spin on names.

After trooping along with the tourist group and straining to understand the tour guide's English, the four of us decided to hang back from the babbling children and loudmouthed tourists for a while. The sexual intrigue was only accentuated when the lights suddenly went out and we were plunged into complete and utter darkness.

We realized that since the tour group had moved on, the energy-conserving Chinese people saw no need to illuminate our section of the cave. I suddenly had a flashback to when I had landed in Beijing the first time. There were bright lights, fountains everywhere, lights and sound. But as the airport emptied out and people found taxis and airport buses, suddenly, on cue, most of the lights went out and the fountains ceased. This was a way to save on electricity, the same as when drivers of cars that met on dark roads would have their headlights off, only to flash them on briefly as they passed each other—as if that sudden blinding light would not cause an accident in and of itself!

As we sat there in the scary yet intimate darkness, Richard and Dick decided to hoot and bird call when the next group of tourists straggled by to see how they would react. However, as the silence and darkness continued, we suddenly wondered if we had been on the last tour for the day. Would we be stuck in the cold and clammy cave for the night?

Eventually, using the flash on Richard's video camera and moving cautiously inch by inch, we made our way out. It seemed curious to us that no one even seemed to notice our absence. That night, over dinner and drinks, we laughed about it and then reluctantly parted ways, because Richard and Dick were to embark on yet another chapter of their round-the-world adventure. We would never see them again. Yet they had reminded us that we were, in fact, still human and yes, still women.

14

The Saga of Two Foreigners and the Luzhou Protestant Church

Fran

"Can nonbelievers attend church?"
"Do you have to be born a Christian in a Christian home to be a Christian?"
"Do you really pray? What do you say when you pray?"
"Why do Christians always say 'God bless me!' Or do they say 'God bless you'?"

SOME OF OUR STUDENTS were keen on peppering us with questions about our religion; they had an insatiable curiosity about what we believed. One of our students, who was 54, told us he had had some foreign teachers before foreigners were expelled from the country. He added, "I attended church as a boy, but since then I have rejected belief in any religion."

Here and there, individuals dared to expose their Christian leanings to us. One young woman who had lived in Indonesia and then returned to her hometown in Luzhou was quite frank about her beliefs and asked many questions about ours. Another young man came up to us and confessed that during the Cultural Revolution, he had often harassed Christians, yelling at them that they were Imperialist lovers and that Christianity only sanctioned cruel acts and invasions. He admitted he used to take part in building bonfires to burn books, particularly religious ones, and had even thrown books in the river. But he had since become a Christian and regretted his past cruelties.

But Christianity was not always such an unfamiliar concept. For example, missionaries from the Canadian Methodist Mission had arrived in Sichuan in the 1890s, setting up a mission in Chengdu. In 1908, some missionaries from that organization took up residence in Luzhou and invited people to services in a house. By 1914, they had built a brick church in Luzhou.[1] This church was still standing, used on Sundays by a fledgling congregation. Fairly soon after arriving in Luzhou, in February 1986, Mary Ann and I made an informal request to Teacher Lin of the foreign affairs office to attend that church that we had first heard about from the director of CEE. We then received word that Teacher Lin and another official from the foreign affairs office had visited the city foreign affairs office to ask permission for us. We were told the city officials had responded with "No hurry."

As of May 22, 1986, four months after arriving in Luzhou, our request was still pending. I explained the situation to my parents this way: "The church feels it has to make everything so special if we go. It takes a lot of effort. And then the townspeople will feel uneasy in their worship if we are there. They would have to usher us up to the front row even though we don't understand Chinese." In hindsight, I can recognize the Communist Party line in these words. I was not jaded at that point and so accepted these reasons at face value. It was only many years later that Mary Ann and I found out that college officials had actually promised our CEE leaders from the get-go that we could attend church in Luzhou. They had said that in China "everyone enjoys freedom of beliefs; there is free choice and no coercion."[2] They had assured Bert Lobe, our director, that CEE teachers "could participate as they decided" and that it would be okay for foreign teachers to attend church in Luzhou on Sundays.

In a June 1986 letter, Mary Ann noted, "We saw the church in Luzhou by chance on a walk the other evening. It is a beautiful old building. Church is on our priority list for requests now. We stopped pushing the idea, but now that I've seen the church, I really want to go to a service."

One day that same month, Mary Ann and I were warmed by an experience of stopping by the church and meeting a religious leader there. The building had whitewashed brick walls and several wooden gabled rooftops, with a small white cross topping the middle one. Above the massive wooden

1. Missionary Society of the Methodist Church, *Our West China Mission*, 217–18.
2. "Summary of Visit," 3.

door were etched Chinese characters, red on a black background. We didn't know exactly what they said. We talked with someone there briefly, but soon had to leave as the empty church filled with curious onlookers, peering around columns to see what these foreigners were doing.

The sanctuary of Luzhou Protestant Church

Then a few months later, in September, after losing patience with the process to get the go-ahead to attend church, we decided to go to a Sunday worship service without permission. We were not sure that this was a wise move. The foreign affairs office was certain to find out about it. We figured we had a good reason because Kathleen Griffin, who lived in Virginia, had written to ask us to report on the church. She was born in Luzhou, China, and had lived there until she was about 13 years old, leaving Luzhou in 1926.

One Sunday we ducked off the main market street into a narrow alleyway, timidly pushed open the door, and entered the lofty hall. It was apparently near the end of the service. About twenty people were there singing "Take Time to Be Holy"—in Chinese, of course. The song was slow, sounding almost like a chant. Almost everyone was over 60 years old. This was, we figured, because the old people had nothing to lose as far as job promotions or privileges went if they attended church. Chances were, though, that in a city like Luzhou, few young people were openly Christians.

We talked to the pastor afterwards in a back room through an interpreter. His answers were guarded, but he was friendly. He told us that the church had been closed during the Cultural Revolution but then had been reopened in 1978. He also told us that the church used to be related to a hospital in Luzhou that had since been turned over to the government; that hospital was the Luzhou Medical College hospital!

Luzhou Protestant Church pastors

We were happy to have gone once to get a look at the place, but we felt there wouldn't be a reason to go again. It seemed to us more Christian to not go to church than to go to church, because of the way the presence of a foreigner changed the situation. We knew that Chinese Christians were rebuilding faith communities, and we figured that they needed to learn from each other's experiences more than from ours.

A week later Zhang Dongni told us that the college leaders did find out and that they had seen us, though we were not supposed to know this.

They were evidently surprised that we had been "so bold" as to go to church without permission. But the leaders were not going to confront us about it, which meant that they would confront the church leaders instead. The church leaders would be requested to ask us to leave if we attempted to go again. We were sorry that the pastor would possibly have to answer some questions about our visit. We weren't sure if we had done the right thing by going unannounced.

Later Bert Lobe noted in a CEE report that this visit had caused some tensions and lack of trust from the city and the college toward us. He wrote, however, that after he explained to the college officials our need and intention to go regularly, "the tension dissipated."[3] Apparently, our Chinese hosts decided to let that battle go. In early December 1986, almost a year after we arrived in Luzhou, the *waiban* gave us official permission to go to church.

We attended the church Christmas party that year. At least a hundred people from the local community had gathered. Some of them were there simply to observe, but others were serious. The party was led mostly by elderly people. They requested that Mary Ann and I sing a song, so we sang "Silent Night, Holy Night." Then they sang some familiar Christmas carols and handed out tiny gifts.

In our subsequent, infrequent visits—sometimes we preferred to just have our own private service of two—we noticed one of the Chinese English teachers in the pews. Teacher Pan often wandered the campus alone; in our chance encounters with him, we could smell *baijiu* on his breath. The other teachers seemed to keep their distance from him. We wondered what Teacher Pan had sacrificed in standing and promotion when he decided to attend church. We also wondered what demons might be in his past to cause him to walk, zombie-like, through his life. Curiously, in the last months of my time in Luzhou, Teacher Pan dropped by my apartment more frequently for conversation, seemingly less restricted in doing so.

In March 1987, we attended church again. About thirty-five people were there. We liked the quiet manner of the pastor. Teacher Pan translated parts of the sermon. "Christians should be patient," the pastor said. Afterward, the elderly pastor chatted with us. He showed us the one English book he still possessed, which was a book from 1900 of translated Sichuan dialect idioms. He explained, "The Red Guards took all of my English books, including my English Bible, during the Cultural Revolution."

3. "Summary of a Conversation," 1.

By April, we had full access to the church. During that time, my parents, Elmer and Phyllis Martens, visited Luzhou. It was not surprising that my father, a former Mennonite pastor and seminary president, asked to go to the Luzhou church on Sunday and to visit the pastor afterwards. Although my father noted the same things we did—especially the slow, dirge-like nature of the hymn singing and the fact that the pastor, in his 80s, needed help from a young pastor to find and read the scripture for the day—he was amazed to even be observing a practicing church in Communist China.

When our students learned that my father had been a pastor, they plied him with questions about religion. Palpable energy, eagerness, and excitement filled the room.

One young man declared, "This is my God!" pointing at himself.

My father quipped, "And how do you like your God?" Everyone laughed, and the tension was dispelled.

Another young woman asked my father, with clear amazement in her voice, "Do you really believe there are *gods* in the *sky*?"

When my father mentioned the Christian admonishment to "Love your enemies," I heard one woman in the crowd mutter, "Impossible!" Considering the hand-to-hand fighting between families in Luzhou during the Cultural Revolution, I certainly could not blame her for her sentiment. I thought about that exchange for some time afterwards.

By the fall of 1987, it was clear that we and the church had a more comfortable relationship. On Teacher's Day, the church gave me a wall hanging. We foreign teachers (now minus Mary Ann, who had returned home after her term) were asked to record Christmas hymns for the members who wanted to practice from October to December in order to sing them well (and hopefully a bit more up-tempo). The church also asked that we give several Christmas performances! We agreed to sing only one song in the end: "What Child Is This?" We were startled to hear scattered applause when we finished. At the end of the service, people with candles filed up to the front to receive their gifts: Christmas towels. It was a lovely service.

In January 1988, I made one of my last visits to the church in Luzhou. The congregation that day was quite large. Midway through the service, the lights and sound went out, but no one reacted and the service went on. I was surprised to see the nine young people who had recently been baptized—including three from our college. These nine sang in choir robes that had been handmade by a woman in the church; they even sang one song in English.

In 2021, Mary Ann and I saw photos posted on a blog written by Connie Wieck, an American who had taught English at a technical college in Luzhou from 2007 to 2019. She is a Methodist Christian who was hosted by the Amity Foundation, a Chinese-led Christian organization sanctioned by the Chinese government, to teach in China. According to her reports and photos, right before the pandemic, the Luzhou Protestant Church had a lot of young people and was active in the community. Connie sang in the church choir. However, Connie won't be returning to be a teacher in Luzhou—or China—any time soon. She learned in early 2023 that the Amity Foundation had closed its English-language-teaching program.[4]

4. Wieck, "Updates from Connie," para. 3.

15

Faith Questions
and the Pursuit of Evidence

Mary Ann

Living in a country where most people professed to be atheist, I wondered whether many Chinese people, particularly those my age, felt a longing for God, maybe even secretly. That kind of wondering caused me to question why I had felt I needed God and whether I still needed God. Shouldn't I feel God's presence even if it was not practical to be a churchgoer in Luzhou? Why didn't I feel God's presence? I repeatedly asked these questions while living in China.

As a preteen, I was comfortable talking to God while delivering papers on my paper route or singing to God while riding my bike on country roads. I had grown up attending a small Mennonite church and had been baptized when I was 16, in accordance with the adult baptism practice of Mennonites. However, I increasingly had doubts about my faith during my senior year of college and the following year. In China, those doubts remained unresolved.

After I returned home from China in 1987, through the hospitality of a Mennonite pastor and his wife—Paul and Joy Versluis—in my hometown, I embraced Christianity. Only years later would I develop a practice of prayer and take annual silent spiritual retreats, which would feed my soul. Those kinds of spiritual disciplines, if practiced sooner, might have helped me to nurture my faith while I was in China.

I sometimes expressed my faith struggles in letters to my parents, whose Mennonite Christian faith was an important part of their identity and life practices. I wrote them the following in September 1986, after a year of living in China and several months before Fran and I got official permission to attend the Luzhou Protestant Church:

> Making the transfer from the church experience in the U.S. to here hasn't been easy. Essentially, I still feel a great need for God, but looking at church activities from a distance and reflecting on their meaning sometimes leaves me at a loss. How much do people feel the need to worship or pray without the influence of other Christians? Without the church institution how should I practice my faith? How important is Christianity to me? Quite frankly, in China from what I see, I wouldn't be one of the bold ones who goes to church, especially in Luzhou.

At age 23, I was looking for evidence that Christianity wasn't only a social construct. I *did* come across evidence. Chinese people who became Christians, even if they didn't always share details about their faith experience with me, indicated that something was missing from the kind of atheism promoted by the Communist Party. I admired how some Chinese people went against the societal and political grain to set foot in a Christian church.

In July 1986, Fran and I stopped for a weekend in Chengdu on our way to Nanjing for language study. I went to church there, and I came across a former student who was attending church for the first time. She said she'd been interested in Christianity and had gotten up the nerve to go despite the peer pressure against it. We went out to lunch and talked about faith. It impressed me that she'd gotten excited about Jesus Christ merely by reading the Bible. Back in my home country, I knew only Christians who had received religious training. Here she was, searching for meaning in the teachings of Jesus without having ever been to Sunday School or church.

Later, toward the end of my two years in China, I revisited that church in Chengdu and encountered another former student, Xu Ying. She had been in the young teachers' class I'd taught at Sichuan Normal University. She was delighted to see me in church and shared that she had become a Christian.

After the service, Xu Ying joined a couple of other foreign teachers and me to eat *jiaozi* and then go to the cinema to watch a movie. In the movie, two young people were being ostracized by a village because of their "capitalist" tendencies. They were forced not to have contact with anyone and had to sweep the streets of the village every day. After 1976 and the end of the Cultural Revolution, the couple tried to forget their suffering and got along with the villagers as if the past had never happened.

Xu Ying said that the movie accurately depicted the events of the Cultural Revolution. Then she added, "We have no time for revenge." Her comment struck me as generous and also Christian. It made an impression on me that the vibrant Xu Ying felt she needed God and had become a Christian.

I found additional evidence that some Chinese people were seeking God in the story of an aspiring theologian in Chongqing. During a visit to Chongqing, our teacher friend Ann Martin invited Fran and me to a private gathering in which a young man named Lu Lang spoke to a group of foreigners about his faith. Lu Lang had been accepted into Nanjing Theological Seminary, but the college in Chongqing where he taught English wouldn't release him to attend.

"My grandmother gave me my first Bible," Lu Lang said. "But she had given it to me by mistake, thinking it was a dictionary. Both books were the same size and color." When Lu Lang's uncle discovered the Bible, he called it a "bad book" and burned it. As a youth, Lu Lang began to ask questions about life and death, and about religion. He studied Taoism, Marxism, and Buddhism. He obtained another Bible, and he became a Christian. "I came to realize that life is too short for quarreling and arguing, and people should try to love each other as the New Testament says," he said.

The English teacher said he believed that as a Chinese Christian, he needed to understand Marxism particularly well in order to reach and challenge Chinese people. He explained that he had been told he had a "low political conscience," which might not bode well for his career or educational opportunities. Lu Lang talked about the government regulations concerning Christianity. He felt the church was very controlled, as the pastors were employees of the government. He critiqued the three-self movement, the effort sanctioned by the government for Chinese people to direct all Christian activities. He felt the official church was too connected with the government for attendees to have a full sense of worship. For example, church leaders were charged with carrying out the "four modernizations," just like everyone else. These were goals set for China by Deng Xiaoping, the country's top leader, to achieve progress in agriculture, industry, defense, and science and technology. Lu Lang claimed that Christians were very dependent on authority figures to be their religious medium and that they were not really following their hearts and deepest beliefs.

In a critique of the typical Sunday sermon, the young man said the message typically followed a formula that could be tolerated by the government: "We must ask God to help us build a better socialist future, to help us get ahead with the four modernizations. We pray for peace in the world." He added, "We are not able to meet in small groups to discuss the Bible."

Lu Lang ministered to my spirit through his testimony. His expression of belief didn't fit the mold I was accustomed to and thus seemed fresh and authentic. Lu Lang appeared to me as the prophets of old might have, speaking the truth about what he felt and had witnessed.

16

A Love Match

MARY ANN

WE RELATED TO ALMOST everyone at Luzhou Medical College through the framework of our classroom and therefore didn't get to know many couples or families. Although we had a lot of meaningful interactions with the students in our intensive English course, we had a hard time making sense of the social dynamics among the Chinese teachers of English at the medical college. It was challenging to make connections with them.

Fran and I took turns teaching a seminar-style class once a week to the medical college's English teachers—about ten of them. Their English was strong, and it was entertaining to go through the script of *Our Town* by Thornton Wilder with each participant reading a part out loud. Discussions, however, usually fell flat. We heard rumors that some of these teachers had been at odds with each other during the Cultural Revolution. The English teachers were intellectuals, a class of Chinese citizens that suffered immeasurably during that violent period when the proletariat had power and intellectuals were despised. Mao Zedong encouraged the Red Guards to attack intellectuals as a way of getting rid of capitalism and traditionalism.

It was to be expected that the classroom climate with the English teachers would be stilted. San Francisco Theological Seminary professor Philip L. Wickeri writes about a window of time after the end of the Cultural Revolution, 1977–1983, as a "period of uncertainty" regarding what kinds of ideas would be accepted in the society:

Hope for the future was tempered by doubts whether a new day would really come to pass. People who had fought with one another were now back in their old neighborhoods and work units, and forced to be together. Former "Red Guards" were again working with those whom they had attacked. There was cautiousness over how much one could really say and to whom. Intellectuals spoke about their "lingering fears" (*xin you yu ji*) that it could happen all over again, and so it was better to stay silent and wait and see.[1]

Wickeri's description captures the cautiousness we sensed among the English teachers at Luzhou Medical College. We wondered: Had some of the English teachers accused others in public political meetings for being "counterrevolutionaries"? This had happened to many people who had once associated with Westerners or who had learned English. We never knew, but we generally didn't feel we were successful in building a sense of community in the classroom with that group. At the same time, at the few social events we participated in with the English teachers outside of the classroom—either planned by them or by us—the atmosphere was lighter, and we were able to engage with each other more naturally and personally. Many of the teachers were fluent in English.

One 40-something couple who attended the English-teacher seminar—Teacher Fu and his wife, Teacher Tang—was always very friendly. They provided warm hospitality to us. Teacher Fu was tall and broad-shouldered and had a round face with a ready smile. Though Teacher Tang was also tall, she had narrow shoulders and was very slender; she seemed fragile, in contrast to her husband. Teacher Tang smiled less frequently and widely than Teacher Fu did.

Teacher Fu was almost giddy when he toasted us in his role as head of the English department for our welcome banquet upon our arrival in Luzhou. Our presence on campus represented an opening of the country— and of the city in which they had chosen to live—that he and Teacher Tang had long awaited and welcomed enthusiastically.

Two months into our first semester, the couple invited us to their apartment for an evening meal. At that point, the only invitation we'd had to someone's home that hadn't been rescinded was from Teacher Lin; it seemed that as a *waiban* official, only Teacher Lin could interact with us as he wished.

---

1. Wickeri, *Reconstructing Christianity*, 201.

I'm not sure whether Teacher Fu's position as director of the English teaching department gave him some clout or if he and Teacher Tang just decided to do what they wanted and the *waiban* decided to let it go. The couple struck me as independent.

During our first visit with Teacher Fu and Teacher Tang, they honored us by serving very special kinds of food. A relative had brought a dried plant from Malaysia, and they had waited for a special occasion to cook it into a soup. They told us that our visit was that special occasion. We, of course, hadn't done anything to deserve such special treatment, but we tried to be gracious and appreciative.

Teacher Tang was the only Cantonese-speaking person I met in Sichuan province. The melodic Cantonese dialect was mostly spoken in the south of China, in the province of Guangzhou. However, Teacher Tang wasn't from Guangzhou. Rather, she had grown up in an overseas Chinese family in Indonesia and had moved to mainland China when she was 17. Her parents still lived in Indonesia, and she had other relatives who lived in Hong Kong. She said that for many years during the period when China was "closed," she hadn't been able to communicate with her family.

For once, I didn't ask a lot of questions. Fran and I just listened to the parts of the story Teacher Tang wanted to tell.

Teacher Tang had met and fallen in love with Teacher Fu when they were English teachers studying in Beijing. As a married couple, they had made their home in mainland China and had endured separation for many years during the Cultural Revolution while Teacher Fu was assigned to work in the countryside. After the Cultural Revolution, the couple said they were happy to settle in Luzhou. The subtext was that they had picked an undesirable location so that they could be together. The government assigned many couples to jobs that forced them to live hundreds of miles away from each other for most of the year. But first and foremost, Teacher Fu and Teacher Tang wanted to stay together.

Teacher Fu and Teacher Tang hosted us another time for a meal before we returned the invitation and invited them to our rooms. By then we considered them to be our favorite English teachers. They seemed so much more comfortable with us than many people, and we felt emotionally attached to them, almost as we would to an aunt and uncle. I attributed our connection to the fact that Teacher Tang had grown up in another country and had experience with cross-cultural communication.

During our third semester in Luzhou, we again had the chance to spend several hours with Teacher Fu and Teacher Tang in their home. They shared with us their concern about their son. They wondered whether he would pass China's college entrance exams, which were extremely competitive. Again, we were struck by their love and respect for each other. They seemed to hang on each word their spouse said. Theirs was a love match.

The final time that Teacher Fu and Teacher Tang invited Fran and me over to their home, they didn't serve gourmet food as they had during our first visit. It was a testament to our friendship that we made and ate a simple meal. Together, we made *chaoshou*, a kind of dumpling. I have a photo from that day of Teacher Tang pressing dough around pork filling to make dumplings, with sunlight streaming through a window on her like in a Vermeer painting. She looks so beautiful to me, because memories of her warm personality have stayed with me long after I experienced her hospitality.

17

Tea Parties for Two:
Managing Monotony

FRAN

MARY ANN AND I were happy to be making Chinese friends, but the fact remained: we were two headstrong American women compelled by our situation to spend a lot of time as a twosome. We needed to be creative to overcome boredom or avoid grating on each other's nerves.

Given that we were making only "official," rather stuffy visits to lychee orchards and stone Buddhas where we sometimes feigned interest in the detailed explanations of the sights—compounded by very limited social interactions with our students—we had to provide our own entertainment. Some of what we came up with illustrates the full extent of the monotony we felt.

Tea Parties for Two: Our parties consisted of a) the preparation and b) the event.

First, we had to make the arduous trek from our mountaintop down to the muddy, raw marketplace to get supplies for our party. Walking past the bloody eels that were pounded and slit open on the rocks, we stopped at the tangerine stand to bargain down a villager looking for an easy sale.

We stepped into the dank, cement-block department store to buy a few stale, cream-filled wafers and some rubbery chocolate. Then we walked back up past the ducks that were being watered, quacking noisily with joy as they were herded down the road. We uncomfortably endured the long stares of the old men, dressed in identical dusty-blue attire, caps or berets on their heads, sitting around in small child-size chairs at a corner teahouse. Tobacco smoke hung in the air, along with rank odors of smoke from coal fires and sewage. After huffing up the 200-plus steps to our courtyard, we took a break, drank water, and surveyed our private tearoom on the first floor of our apartment. We laid out our spread, heated some water in an electric kettle, got out our teacups, and voila! We were ready to party!

We ran upstairs to our bedrooms, got into our "party" clothes (a nice sweater, perhaps a cute pair of socks) and put on our music, such as the Talking Heads's "Burning Down the House." With an offer of "Would you like to dance?" and an answer of "Don't mind if I do!", the event was off to a flying start.

Half of our party was figuring out slow *taiji* moves for our "Burning Down" song—a hilarious and incompatible mixture, we thought. Once we had a routine down, it was time for refreshments. We collapsed on the couch, steeped our tea, and lingered over our sumptuous food. After that, it was time to find a topic to debate, which we did with gusto, unable to run to the internet, which hadn't yet been invented, to find facts to prove ourselves right. A few more snacks, a few more sips of tea, and our party was over. Time to take ourselves upstairs to bed.

Movies: We had no Internet, no YouTube—only enigmatic, slow-moving Chinese TV, which often lingered on a single white blossom or bird for five–ten seconds before moving on. Despite its agonizing, glacier-like pace, we actually watched the entire forty-some episodes of *Wu Zetian*, a historical, literary Masterpiece Theater of China about an empress in the Tang Dynasty.

Mostly, we read a lot of books. I enjoyed reading O'Henry short stories. Mary Ann's favorite was *The Adventures of Huckleberry Finn*; she saw a connection between Huck Finn's life on the Mississippi and the life of local fishing families on the Yangtze.

We also carefully rationed out the cassette tapes that family and friends sent our way—Garrison Keillor, Fleetwood Mac, Joan Baez, Joni Mitchell, and Paul Simon. We did not want to get tired of them, and we knew it would be a long time before another batch of tapes came in.

We liked reading, but nonetheless we waited impatiently for the next movie to come to campus, which happened about once a month. What would it be this time? Another propagandistic Chinese film? A trigger-happy gangster who shot up his enemies without remorse, a sordid love affair with a loose American woman, a martial arts movie with swords and incredible flips in the air? After one or two of these movies, we realized the best we were going to get was a B movie with a ridiculous plot and a lot of violence. We hadn't even known that they made movies this bad!

The movie "theater" was a room in the center of campus with about 200 uncomfortable wooden seats and mountains of sunflower-seed shells between the aisles to gingerly step over. Moviegoers liked to eat not popcorn but sunflower seeds during movies, which was unfortunate because particularly during quiet scenes, one could hear the sound, all over the theater, of the spitting out of shells onto the floor. That and seemingly inappropriate laughter at the emotional parts, if there were any (laughter often meant embarrassment) caught us by surprise. Of course, a major distraction was that the movies were dubbed in Chinese. We had to use our imaginations to fill in the plot. Or we had an interpreter.

Although we did not care for the movie selection, there was actually one Chinese film, made in 1986, called *In the Wild Mountains*, that seemed to us to be a brilliant, accurate depiction of Chinese rural life. I was pleased to recognize some familiar elements, like kids in split pants; men on their haunches, gossiping; the subtle cues of couples that meant love. The story was surprising—basically a couple exchange. I wrote, "Divorce and remarriage that was pictured in the film is not condoned here—yet the picture was shown. Why? We are not sure except that the picture of Chinese life and culture was so excellently done and photography excellent. Also, it showed the betterment of Chinese peasant life—a popular topic now."

As for American films, we saw *First Blood* and *Superman*. We also saw a lot of foreign films—from Japan, Hong Kong, Germany, and Brazil. China seemed to be loosening up some.

On pre-arranged days—so our interpreter or a representative from the *waiban* could come over and keep tabs on the conversation—small groups of students were allowed to come over in the evening for tea. They liked to hear our music tapes and were particularly attracted to James Taylor.

Once, on April 1, to illustrate April Fools' Day, I turned on the tape recorder in class, supposedly to start a dialogue in English, but instead to blast out Whitney Houston's "How Will I Know." Also on April 1, for the amusement of ourselves and our students, Mary Ann and I traded the outfits that we wore day in and day out and tried to imitate each other's mannerisms in class until our students caught on, and then we could explain the American April Fools' Day.

Mooncakes: An annual event, the Harvest Moon Festival provided a convenient excuse for students to come by and drop off mooncakes. We loved the sentimental, nostalgic poetry that students would recite, such as one about two lovers looking at the same moon from a great distance, separated by war or other circumstances.

But something we did not relish about the festival was the ubiquitous, heavy, doughy mooncakes filled with red beans. After school events where we had mooncakes as the featured item, we ended up with well-meaning gifts of stacks of mooncakes from students and teachers, more than we knew what to do with.

One night, shortly after the Harvest Moon Festival, the two of us bought a dusty plum wine bottle of some unknown origin at the local convenience shop on the side of the hill on campus. Setting out our wine and mooncakes—upstairs on the back balcony this time, to be well out of the way of any prying eyes—we relaxed, enjoying the view of a hillside of trees sloping down to the streets of the town. We told each other the funniest, most embarrassing stories of our lives while getting tipsy and nibbling on mooncakes. The hills rang out with our laughter. Perhaps the locals were wondering whether these foreign "ghosts" were in fact truly going crazy.

Photo Shoots: Another way we relieved our boredom, especially on Sunday afternoons, was to wander around the picturesque campus and take pictures of each other. We dressed up and emulated the Chinese women at tourist sites who had confident poses. We laughed and joked as we posed. The film rolls had to be sent back to the United States to be developed; we did not see our final products until much later.

Mary Ann in stone garden   **Fran in field of flowers**

Writing Letters: We spent hours each week writing letters by hand on semitransparent rice paper. Our letters to our parents, friends, and family served as open personal journals of our wonderings and emotional ups and downs. It was almost impossible to have a dialogue. The problem was that a question in one letter would take nearly a month to receive an answer (two weeks to get to its destination and then two more weeks for a response letter). By then, we hardly remembered the original issue or question!

I got impatient with the slow pace of these conversations, especially with my boyfriend, Ken, who was writing from Lesotho. So I tried phone calls. That was an onerous process. First, I went with an interpreter to the local operator halfway across campus. I would arrange a time to try to make a phone call abroad. Then, I would rush back to our tearoom and wait for the operator to connect with an operator in the eastern part of the country, likely Beijing, who would then relay the call. The phone would eventually ring at our place. I would pick it up to hear a lot of static and the distant, crackly voice of a loved one. Usually, we got cut off somewhere in the middle of the call. A slightly better connection could be had by going down to the post office, paying for a call in advance, and then waiting until one's number came up for a particular phone booth. That, of course, was even more of a hassle. Ken and I realized we had completely underestimated the difficulties of communicating between our locations in two countries that had limited communication technologies.

Mary Ann didn't call anyone outside of China ever. She tried once to arrange a call with the local operator on campus to call her parents on an American holiday. The call didn't go through; she never tried again.

Neighborly Nosiness: Our living quarters were sandwiched in between two prominent Luzhou families. The family on our right was reserved but friendly. Since they did not speak English nor we much Chinese, we did not interact much. We once received an invitation to the 1-year-old birthday party of a newborn (considered 1 year old at birth). It was a rare social event, albeit just next door; we were thrilled. However, we were a bit chagrined when, after we complimented our neighbors on their living room décor of peacock feathers, they pulled one down from the wall and gave it to us! I think that they might have felt sorry for us, so far away from home and family. It was also the local custom to give guests something if they profusely admired it.

One of two sets of twins in our neighborhood. Parents were elated when they had twins because it was a way to get around the one-child-only policy in the 1980s.

On the other side of us was a very inquisitive, smiley neighbor woman with a round face. We at first welcomed the diversion of chatting with someone other than each other, since she knew some English and seemed to like engaging us in conversation. She was often outdoors, sweeping the courtyard or hanging laundry, when we would step out, so we chatted on a regular basis. At some point, though, we got annoyed at her seemingly endless curiosity about where we were going when we left the building. She also wanted to know when we expected to return, whether we were going with someone, what we were going to buy—the questions went on. It dawned on us, finally, that she must be a designated informer, the one who would keep tabs on what the foreigners were up to. This woman was among the ranks of our knitting interpreter and the family member of a random medical student, who blurted out upon meeting us: "Oh, I know who you are! My brother is your bodyguard!" We hadn't known that we had bodyguards!

Though it seemed others were watching out for us, it was in a dispassionate way; we were left with the realization that for intimacy and support, we would simply need to watch out for each other. Making sense of everything was confusing, and we took comfort in processing life in Luzhou together.

18

A Christmas Party and News of Shanghai Student Protests

MARY ANN

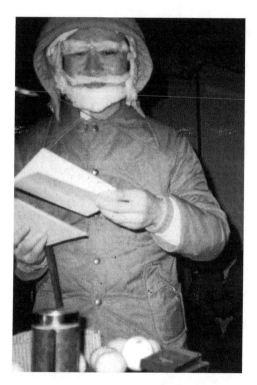

Our Christmas party gets a surprise guest: Santa Claus!

Our students planned a Christmas party for us because they didn't want us to feel homesick. A few days before, on December 21, tens of thousands of students had marched in Shanghai calling for "democracy" and freedom of the press after student protests had been initiated in the cities of Hefei and Wuhan. Encouraged by some progressive elites at universities and seeing possible openness by the government, the students called for more say in elections within the socialist system. At first a spokesperson for the Shanghai city government said the protests were "legal."[1] But by December 23, after an estimated fifty thousand people had demonstrated in Shanghai on the previous day, the Shanghai police banned any future protests.[2] Fran and I didn't have timely access to news about current events, so as was the case with almost everything, we first learned about the protests from our students. I tried to capture the Christmas-party experience with imagery in a poem.

Christmas Party in Luzhou

They came with shiny hair
in crisp suits
cleverly hiding winter layers.

Forty people sang
"Silent Night" by candlelight
and we two foreigners
presented the "Gift of the Magi."
The food was richer than usual
so the rice-fed Santa Claus gained some needed weight.
Guests laughed, danced, and
cracked sunflower seeds.
They threatened not to go home
until everyone had given a performance
(the Tibetan dancers were a hard act to follow).
Amid the uproar
a middle-aged man softly told me
youth in Shanghai had gathered by the thousands
to demand freedom.
His voice sang as if he were passing on
holiday cheer.

1. Gargan, "Thousands."
2. Gargan, "Warning."

19

Impressions of Indiana from a Chinese Educator

FRAN

ONE OF THE MIDDLE-AGED English teachers who had attended our weekly seminar was selected to study in Indiana at Goshen College, our alma mater, for a year. CEE was a teacher–scholar exchange program. Each year, CEE sponsored a small number of Chinese faculty from the same Chinese institutions that employed North American English teachers (such as Mary Ann and me) to study English at Mennonite colleges in the United States. Teacher Bai stayed in the house of a legendary music teacher at Goshen College: Mary Oyer. In November 1986, Teacher Bai wrote a letter that addressed us as a unified person. The letter was warm and friendly.

> Dear Frances and Mary Ann,
>
> Very glad to hear from you both. With your letter in my hands, I shouted, jumped, kissed it, and laughed. I felt so dear and so excited when reading the letter. I am so happy to know that you are getting along very well with your work. You are enjoying your life there because you are becoming more and more familiar with both the people and surroundings there. I'm happy too that you are not as busy as last term. What fascinates me most is that you are now working hard at your Chinese, and Mary Ann even can write several Chinese characters very well. I hope when I meet you next time, you can greet me in Chinese!

Dear Frances and Mary Ann, I'm so glad that you toured around south and east of China. I also went there a few years ago. You will miss those places long, long after your tour. Are you going to do some traveling this coming winter vacation? How about your teaching program? Are you both still going to teach in my college? How I hope you can stay there until I come back and we can work together, or you come back and meet me here in Goshen. Anyhow I hope you can do whatever pleases you.

As to me, I am getting along well. My study is going smoothly. I'm now used to the life and surroundings here. I have my host family and some other American friends. They are very kind and helpful to us. Every Saturday we go shopping in Kmart, in JCPenney, or in Kroger. At the end of last month we went to Detroit and had a very nice time there. We went to the top of the Renaissance building and have a wonderful overview of both Detroit and the part of Canada across the Detroit River. There we visited the art museum, were interviewed by the WJR radio station. I also got a chance to go to a wedding. Oh, my goodness. It's too long for me to present you all my experience there. The middle of this month we went to Columbus to attend the TESOL conference there.

But I dare say I don't like Columbus, which is much worse than Goshen. In Goshen people have beautiful houses surrounded by lawns, trees, and flowers, and have nice houses for cars too. But in Columbus the houses are too crowded, no lawn, no flowers, few trees. The cars are sadly sitting along the roadsides, taking the wind, the rain, the snow as their companies. Oh, I like Goshen and miss Goshen whenever I leave it for other places.

We have nice time with our American friends, observing Halloween and Thanksgiving with them. I made a Jack-o-Lantern in my host family's house and had turkey in several friends houses. We also cook some Chinese food for them. I am so glad that our American friends always like Chinese food, especially Sichuan food. So I think it would be better for you to learn how to cook several Chinese dishes. When you come back, then you can cook Chinese food to treat your friends and they will admire you.

Well, I have so many things to tell you. Anyhow I have to stop here.

Best wishes.
Sincerely your,
Bai Yu

When Teacher Bai arrived back in Luzhou, she would sometimes tell me stories about her time in the United States when she went walking with me. One tale that surprised me was about the time she hitchhiked to and from Kmart with other Chinese teachers!

Teacher Bai also discussed with me her own observations about gender roles in the United States. For example, she told me, "I think the U.S. is a man's world. The men always say, 'Ladies first,' but this is just an overcoat for 'Men first.'" This comment made me think of the skepticism Mary Ann and I had about the Chinese phrase we often heard: "Women hold up half the sky."

Teacher Bai also told me that she found it intriguing that in the United States she dreamed in color, whereas in China she dreamed in black-and-white. When I reported Teacher Bai's experience with her dreams to Mary Ann, she put her own spin on it in a poem.

Dreaming at Different Longitudes

In China
she dreams
only in neutral
since Liberation by Communists
a shaking down of colors
engulfed all
in socialist cement gray
which endures
even in the subconscious.

But in capitalist America,
objects and people
vying, screaming for attention
appear in garish color
in her dreams.

20

On the Other Side of the Looking Glass: Wandering China

FRAN

AFTER EVERY SEMESTER, MARY Ann and I were granted a generous break of a few weeks to wander around the country. During the slow-paced periods of life in Luzhou, we planned out our upcoming Spring Festival or summer travels in great detail and with growing excitement. These vacation times gave us not only amazing adventures but also a chance to escape the lockdown of Luzhou and get out from under the constant scrutiny of those who had jurisdiction over us. We imagined that once we walked out the gates of the college, those same authorities breathed a sigh of relief because they were no longer responsible for us.

We loved blending in with other backpacker travelers and visiting prominent sites of attraction around China: the Great Wall, the Guilin limestone mountains, and the Xi'an terracotta warriors. However, oddly enough, when we traveled, we were demoted to one of the lower tiers of foreigners. That was because we had a teaching card that allowed us to pay in *renminbi* (Chinese currency) instead of FEC, the more coveted "foreign money." Using *renminbi* put us decidedly lower than big-buck tourists, so when we looked for rooms at hotels, the standard answer was *meiyou* (not have). Sometimes it literally left us stranded late at night. We learned to hide our backpacks behind pillars in hotel lobbies, freshen up, and try to look well-off when approaching the reception desk.

The two of us had already had a taste of traveling together in China, as we had visited Yunnan Province before settling into Luzhou. When we looked back at that first trip, Mary Ann and I realized that Yunnan Province in Southwest China was everything Luzhou was not—sunny, wide, spacious, exotic, and tropical. The weather was perfect, a balmy seventy degrees Fahrenheit. We ended up in a fifteen-person dormitory. We washed clothes, hung them on the roof, and then lounged around, writing postcards and soaking in the sun.

After several forays into the Yunnan city of Kunming to see parks, the Bamboo Temple, Dragon Gate, and the Stone Forest, we traveled down to Xishuangbanna, a much-talked-about region where various minority groups lived. Although we enjoyed the fresh vegetables (fried grass and moss), fish, and soups there and drank in the colorful early market scenes, we felt distinctly uncomfortable on one of our arranged day trips. A group of us foreigners was herded into a bus and taken out to a Hani minority village. As the leader of the tour talked to us through his bullhorn, we stumbled through the village, acutely aware of our foreignness as we stared at women dressed in black clothes embellished with bright red and yellow embroidery, weaving bits of cloth on wooden looms, hushing crying babies, and tending to the pigs snuffing in the hay beneath stilt houses. The men were out gathering wood or working in the fields, we were told. The villagers all tried to ignore the tour group, as if there were not these tall, white, strangely dressed foreigners with big cameras pointed at their every move. Mary Ann and I couldn't bear to take any photos, so we didn't, and we were relieved when we could leave, clambering over the wooden-slatted, rickety bridge and heading back to the bus. The two of us sat in uneasy silence as we made our way back to the hotel. It felt wrong—very, very wrong—to see the Han Chinese people, China's majority group, exploiting minority groups for tourism. We had been required to pay U.S. dollars for the trip. We were both glad to be leaving that region the next day.

Mary Ann and I decided for the Spring Festival holiday of 1987 to go to the famous Hainan Island in the South China Sea, both because it sounded exotic and because we would get to launch from Hong Kong, a place that I remembered as decadent—as in clean, shiny, and rich.

◦ ◦ ◦

Spring Festival incorporates Chinese New Year and is like Thanksgiving, Christmas, and every other major American holiday rolled into one. It is a time when the constant activity, construction, marketplace wrangling, blaring of horns, and general hustle and bustle come to a screeching halt (except for the loud beer-induced singing and small firecrackers that children love to throw at people's feet in the streets). It is a time when cities empty out, and people travel home to the villages where they were born, hold big family feasts, and give children little red envelopes with money— hence the Christmas-like, festive air and excitement. It is a time when all of China seems to be on the move.

The first part of our trip that spring of 1987 was daunting. After a mountainous bus ride to the packed city of Chongqing, we had to take a seventy-hour train ride to Guangzhou (Canton), essentially going from the southwest to the southeast. Even with help from a *waiban* in Chongqing, it was difficult to get tickets, since that trip was a popular route for Chinese people in the winter. When we got to Chongqing, we were surprised and disappointed to realize we only had tickets for halfway to our destination and for hard seats. This was the lowest of the classes of tickets, which were classified in order of comfort: hard seat, soft seat, hard sleeper, and soft sleeper. We spent a day in Chongqing changing the tickets to ones that would take us all the way to Guangzhou, but they were still for hard seats.

Hard seat, the lowest of several classes on the train

In the crowded and dirty train station, we made our way to our seats, walking among squatting children and caged chickens in the aisles. We first had to deal with people already sitting in our thinly padded, wooden, no-nonsense seats. After dealing with immense confusion, the language barrier between us, and general discussion around us, the couple got up and left us the seats. The seats were double-booked because apparently a train had broken down, and the people on that train had climbed aboard this one. People in the train car were quarreling, and one physical fight broke out as people vied for seats. We sank into our seats with relief and shut our eyes, willing the noise, bickering, and shuffling around us to recede.

After people had settled down, Mary Ann decided to try to find the conductor to upgrade our tickets. We knew that the soft sleeper option, with cushiony accommodations, had a closed door to the general aisle that ran down one side of the train, *and* that that configuration could spell trouble if we were trapped with hard-smoking, seed-spitting cadres. So we aimed to buy tickets for hard sleeper. The berths, with minimal padding, were stacked on both sides of a compartment that was open to the aisle; these were usually quite dirty but airier.

I stayed behind with the luggage and to make sure that we didn't lose the seats we had. It took Mary Ann an hour to squeeze past people in the aisles of eight train cars to find the conductor. The wait seemed like forever. I witnessed one mother whistling to her baby so he could pee through his slit pants in the aisle. Because we were foreigners, Mary Ann experienced no difficulty in changing the tickets to hard sleeper. Rather than force her way back through the crowded train, she waited until the train made a stop, jumped off, and sprinted down the platform to the car where I was holding the seats. I tossed our luggage out the train window and Mary Ann sprinted halfway back toward the car with the hard-sleeper seats before jumping back on the train. I made my way through the aisles to meet up with Mary Ann.

At that point we were surprised and pleased to run into one of our students (who was in the hard-seat section) and chatted with him in the aisle for about an hour. He was going back to his hometown to celebrate the New Year with his family. We still had several train cars to go before reaching the car with the hard-sleeper seats. So when the train stopped once again, we jumped off the train, ran to the car with our new seats, and hopped back on the train. We could have been left on the platform, but we took the risk, and we made it!

A couple of hours into the trip, we were feeling more settled, sitting in a four-person compartment across from an American traveler and a young Chinese businessman. The businessman kept to himself, reading newspapers or sleeping most of the time. The American, Dennis, had strawberry blond hair, a grizzly beard, a lithe body, and a friendly demeanor. He had just finished a two-year stint in Kenya with the Peace Corps and was also on his way to Hong Kong. We struck up a lively conversation with Dennis and enjoyed his company for the remainder of the trip, chatting from time to time, reading, sleeping, and staring out the window as the cultivated rice fields flew by. For the next sixty-eight hours, time stood still. It was just what we needed. I spent hour after hour immersed in a new book that my friends had sent: *Zen and the Art of Motorcycle Maintenance*. It was the perfect thing for the liminal space we were in, temporarily disconnected from both our American and our Chinese lives, with no idea where we were at any given time, floating in a time warp. I resonated with the Eastern philosophy I saw enacted before my eyes. Time was not linear, life was a circle, all was connected.

The last ten hours, however, got grueling. We were tired, hot, and longing for a good shower and a comfy bed. We appreciated the hot-water thermos provided for every compartment that we could use for steaming cups of tea and hot ramen, but our snacks of chocolate and chips were now gone, and we three were getting grumpy and short with each other. In addition, there were black flakes of coal from the steam engine in our hair; when we blew our noses, the phlegm came out black. And the bathrooms with squat toilets through which we could see the tracks below were getting unbearably smelly.

At last we arrived and stumbled off the train, taking a moment to regain our land legs, feeling the train's movement still in our bodies. After securing one room for all three of us in thrifty backpacking style at a downtown hostel in Guangzhou and taking a blessed, blessed shower there, the three of us headed off to the best meal we could find—in the swanky White Swan Hotel. Dennis was now an integral part of our party and a great traveling companion. We ordered spaghetti there, since we could not afford anything fancier. Dennis did not think his coffee was warm enough and ordered it back to the kitchen. We gasped. But we were even more surprised when he asked for Parmesan cheese—and they had it! We could not believe the luxury. Were we still in China?

The next morning, crossing by speed train over the border at Shenzhen, the new Economic Zone, into British Hong Kong, our eyes blurred at the shiny lights, modern buildings, garish billboards, beautiful harbor, stuff, stuff, stuff in the stores. Anything you could imagine! Watches, cameras, gadgets, clothes, jewelry. We checked in at a stuffy little hotel in the midst of this consumer madness, collapsed in the beds, and napped for a few hours. The next day Dennis dragged us to a movie, *Aliens*, in which an alien head popped out of Sigourney Weaver's stomach (we identified a bit with the alien), and then we ate at Pizza Hut. Mary Ann headed off with Dennis to the high-rise apartment of a rich woman he had met on the street, and I got a luxurious haircut in a salon where the haircutter massaged my head for quite some time. Heaven!

Several delicious dinners later, with precious few dollars in our pockets and loaded with our purchases of Casio watches, new clothes, and a Nikon camera (yes, we succumbed to the allure of stuff), we affectionately said goodbye to Dennis and went on our own way: to Hainan Island, a tropical island with gorgeous beaches, warm water, and sunny skies, which were especially welcome because they were so often elusive in Luzhou.

PART II:
Deepening Understanding

21

Student Protests and the Ouster of a National Leader

Mary Ann

At the Christmas party in Luzhou, before Fran and I had taken off on our travels to the south during the Spring Festival in the beginning of 1987, students had told us surreptitiously that something political was afoot in China. They wanted us to know they saw it as a big deal that students had demonstrated by the tens of thousands in Shanghai and other cities for democracy. Fran and I didn't ever bring up the words "freedom" or "democracy" in our teaching or discussions with students. We were in China to learn about how the government and society operated there, not to discuss the merits or demerits of our own political system.

Occasionally students commented directly on the economic and political systems of the United States. They expressed the idea that capitalism breeds corruption. "It seems like many U.S. administrations have troubles eventually," observed one middle-aged student. He bolstered his observation with the examples of Watergate and the Iran–Contra affair, the latter of which had just been reported in the news. After the United States bombed Libya in April 1986, a couple of students made a point of telling us they opposed that aggression. So did we, we responded. As Mennonites, we were pacifists.

Our students spoke positively of former U.S. president Richard Nixon because he had been partly responsible for the reopening of China to the

West. As for Ronald Reagan, the man who was the U.S. president then, a couple of students who talked politics for an evening with us in our tea-room thought his domestic policy made sense but that he was too power-hungry internationally.

It was through our Chinese students that I first learned about many historical events featured in their education, such as the raping and looting by Japanese soldiers in 1937 in the city of Nanjing. Even though the United States had been the enemy of China during the Korean War in the 1950s, our students were more likely to be critical of Japan than of the United States. One student once told us that he hated Japan and couldn't forgive the Japanese for the atrocities they had committed when Japan invaded China.

China was at war with Vietnam in the mid-1980s. Back in Chengdu, I'd seen students at Sichuan Normal University carry banners on their way to the train tracks located near the university. They would cheer for and bestow gifts on Chinese soldiers who were being transported by train to the front lines near Vietnam.

In Luzhou, students' writing provided some insight into their country's systems. We came to recognize certain ideas of the Communist Party because they were repeated often. Students lauded China's development projects, mentioned the "four modernizations," praised the sincerity and honesty of Communist Party members, and stressed the necessity of maintaining good personal physical health to benefit the socialist republic. Students reported that China had a lack of good health care "before Liberation," when Communists took control of China, and noted that the country had an abundance of hospitals "after Liberation."

No one from Luzhou Medical College ever told us that the hospital connected with the college had been founded by the Canadian Methodist Mission decades "before Liberation." It was the pastor at the Luzhou Protestant Church who told us that fact. A missionary doctor sponsored by the mission, named Richard Wolfendale, moved to Luzhou in 1915, and he took charge of a new brick dispensary with twenty-five beds.[1] Wolfendale wrote, "The first half-year of 1916 the inpatient total was about 280, and we had them lying in consulting room, waiting room, etc., . . . on boards and straw on the floor, packed like herrings,—mostly wounded soldiers!"[2] He explained that the fighting then was between people from Yunnan Province and "Northerners," with the soldiers from Yunnan ultimately taking

1. Missionary Society of the Methodist Church, *Our West China Mission*, 400.
2. Missionary Society of the Methodist Church, *Our West China Mission*, 222.

control of Luzhou that year. Although some people we interacted with on campus might have known this history, it wasn't politically correct in the 1980s for Chinese people to mention missionaries or mission dispensaries or hospitals.

Sometimes a student reached back into the past to respond to a composition prompt. Events of the Cultural Revolution sometimes made their way into student essays. For example, one student wrote about the death of Mao Zedong, who had died on September 9, 1976:

> That day, it was cloudy, I was laboring in the field with some peasants digging and having a joke. However, everybody had a little fun. It seems to me that something would happen. While having a rest, I went to the stream and sat on a stone. As I was looking at the water thinking of nothing, suddenly a young man cried in the verge of the crowd: "Come back! Quickly come back. There is important news to broadcast." I stood up and went home. When I got near my house, I was surprised at a mournful song, it was told us a leader of our country had been died. "Who? Who has been died?" I hardly dare to guess. A sorrowful and bitter voice came over. "The Chairman of Central Committee of the Communist Party of China; The Chairman of the Military Commission of the Central Committee of the Chinese Communist Party. . . . "
>
> I was frightened out of my wits and could not move and think for an instant! A few minutes later, I heard many many peasants crying. Tears dropped down from my face instantly. I would never forget today when people's great savior Mao Zedong was died.

Another student wrote about the fall of the Gang of Four, a group of leaders from the original Communist revolution that included Mao Zedong's wife. The Gang of Four became a scapegoat for the ills of the Cultural Revolution soon after Mao Zedong died. Removal of the Gang of Four from power officially marked the end of the Cultural Revolution. The change in power at the top signaled that intellectuals, who had been ostracized, would be reinstated in society. The student wrote:

> It was a nice day. I strolled toward the school. Without school discipline, we were free on October 10, 1976. Although I was a child, I was surprised at a piece of news which was announcing that the Gang of Four was overthrown. During that time, I saw many teachers jumping up happily. Many people, including teachers, students and workers, marched on the street, holding up flags and shouting loudly dialogs. While I was standing at the side of street, there crowded people, noise. In that evening, I went to see

the play which congratulated on having overthrown the Gang of Four. After having a dinner, the whole country was in happiness. That day was a significant historical day, since that time our country has made a great progress.

The political winds toward openness in the 1980s abruptly changed direction soon after the student protests at the end of 1986. In January 1987, Hu Yaobang, the general secretary of the Communist Party, was ousted from his position because some more conservative party leaders considered him to have been soft on the students who had taken to the streets in December.

One of our students was particularly concerned about the removal of Hu Yaobang from power. When we had spontaneously met him on the train traveling from Chongqing to Guangzhou for our Spring Festival vacation, he had expressed worry about the implications of Hu Yaobang's ousting. He had just kept shaking his head and saying despondently, "This is bad. This is very bad." The student had also reminded us in that conversation that politics permeated everyday life. He broke the news there on the train that he had been denied the chance to study in the intensive English program with Fran and me for a second semester. He said it didn't matter that he had one of the top scores on the admissions test. The student speculated that the denial was because he had been so friendly with us. He said one of his classmates hadn't said a word to us when he had been in our class, and he had been given the opportunity to join the upcoming English class. We felt a dull emptiness to learn that our English teaching was possibly being used to elevate some promising students and put down others.

During our travels, I read about the ousting of Hu Yaobang in the English *China Daily* and in newspapers in Hong Kong. Several other intellectuals in the party had also been denounced along with him. The Chinese press talked about the problem of "bourgeois liberalization," which the Chinese Communist Party defined as "negating the socialist system and favoring the capitalist system."[3] I read that "bourgeois liberalization" had asserted its influence, and the government had tried to clear up this problem. I wondered whether people in Luzhou would react to the hardliners' response by being even more reluctant than they already were to interact with Fran and me. That would be discouraging for us.

Fran and I weren't aware of any specifics of the political demonstrations at the time, but the Chinese Communist Party responded to the

3. Madsen, "Spiritual Crisis," 246.

1986 student protests with a campaign against "bourgeois liberalism" that crushed the hopes of many intellectuals. Richard Madsen, an American sociologist specializing in China, visited China and interviewed about fifty Chinese intellectuals in late 1988 about what challenges had been created by China's reforms and opening to the world. Intellectuals had embraced reforms with hope and joy and felt that the 1986 campaign against "bourgeois liberalism" was a regression in politics. Madsen wrote, "A decade after the reforms were launched, it was apparent to many of them that most of the people who had gained real control over the Chinese government did not respect, value, trust, or listen to intellectuals."[4]

Though Fran and I often analyzed what we heard about politics in our conversations with each other, we struggled to make sense of it all. Fran and I both underestimated the extent to which Hu Yaobang would be made into a hero by Chinese students at elite universities, and how the hardliners would counter the students' desire for political change. Hu Yaobang's death in 1989 provided a catalyst for masses of students to take to the streets demanding "freedom" and "democracy." Those protests in support of Hu Yaobang led to the occupation of Tiananmen Square by students in 1989.

Fran in Tiananmen Square in 1986

4. Madsen, "Spiritual Crisis," 250.

22

A Modern Chinese Woman

FRAN

ONE OF THE CHINESE English teachers we taught in our weekly seminar stood out immediately to us. Teacher Lu was about our age and had a confident, sophisticated, world-wise manner. She had a dry, sarcastic sense of humor and a sassy haircut to match. Her sense of fashion was much more to Western taste, with tasteful and colorful blouses, not the drab blues and browns commonly worn. For instance, on a picnic for the English teachers one time, she was striking in an attractive, loosely knitted, burnt-orange sweater worn with black pants. We were impressed by her and felt a bit dowdy in her presence.

One time when we asked the English teachers what topics they would like us to discuss with them during their seminar, Teacher Lu said, "Modern life in America." But I imagine she read us well and surmised that we were not a very "modern" representation of America!

Teacher Lu's English was fluent, and we knew by her comments during the seminar for English teachers that she had read a number of the Western classics. She was knowledgeable about such American authors as Hemingway, Fitzgerald, and Dickinson. She was much younger than the rest of the faculty and was the quickest to answer our questions in the once-a-week seminar.

Teacher Lu interacted with us only on her own terms. She didn't fawn over us or seek us out before or after the seminar. One reason she was not wowed by us was that she had studied English with a number of foreign teachers in Chongqing, where she'd lived before being assigned to Luzhou. At that time, Chongqing had about eleven million people.

On rare occasions, while Mary Ann and I were out walking, Teacher Lu approached us to strike up a conversation. Once we conversed about the customs concerning the dead.

"When the government made it mandatory for everyone to cremate bodies rather than bury them, how did people respond?" Mary Ann asked.

"There was no reaction," Teacher Lu said. "Some people just continue to bury bodies in secret." Then she told us a story. "Last month my friends lost their grandfather. His family took him into the country and buried him without telling anyone. They told everyone they had burned the body. The old people in China believe that the spirit will live longer if bodies are buried."

Then she had a question for us. "I had a foreign teacher once who told me that she believed in God and when people die their spirits go up to heaven. Do you believe that?"

Mary Ann responded. "I believe in God. I think there is someone or something in life and death that is more than ourselves. I don't think much about heaven or hell, or worry about it, but I think that after people die, something good happens to them."

"Like what?"

"I don't know what exactly, but something."

"Teacher Lu, do you think the spirit dies with the body?" I interjected.

"Yes," she said without any hesitation.

Another time when we chanced to meet Teacher Lu on a walk, she confessed that she preferred life in a large city to life in Luzhou. She said that when she danced disco in Luzhou at dance parties, people said bad things about her. (Ballroom dancing was the rage at the dance parties in Sichuan, not freestyle dancing to disco music or rock 'n' roll.) Teacher Lu said that sometimes if she felt sad and frustrated, she would close herself up in her room, play music, and "dance like mad." I got the sense that she was like a firefly, trapped in a jar with nowhere to go.

23

Students Write
about Family Dynamics

SOME RESPONSES TO AN essay prompt about "China's generation gap" by students in the spring 1987 intensive English course:

At first glance, you see the young and old live under the same roof and the family are all happy to live together. That's true but under the same roof there are still some different opinions between the generations. Usually, it is the old who complain their children depend on them too much. In many families today, the grandparents, who have retired from hard work of several decades, have to shoulder the responsibility to take care of grandchildren. They have to do all the housework and sometimes they have to spend their pension supporting their children's family. In contrast the young sometimes don't understand the old. They don't like to do housework and they don't even know how to take care of their own children. So people often worry about the young. It is often wondered how the young can live if without the old people's help.

ᘓᘉᘎᘍ

Next door, I often heard the family has argument the young with his father over political point of view. The young who has just come back from the U.S.A. says we ought to learn from all of advanced somethings, especially some advanced political system in order to make our old country further reformed. We ought to take off all old idea. His father argue with his son. He said, "We ought to change our rate slowly and try to keep more customs. We don't like competition cruelty in western countries."

From my neighbor's arguments I made out the young people have high spirit and brave idea. We must realize today's China should need much more people who should have new idea and (reactive) spirits because young people represent our future.

\ᦂ/

It is reported more and more young couples would like to live alone where not far from their parents' home. Why? Do the young resent the old? No, but between the young and old people there is rather a difference in some major points of opinion and life-style. . . . A young surgeon said: At the first time we marriage, we lived together with my parents. Of course, my parents gave us many helps, but my wife and my mother sometimes quarreled for some small things. For examples, my wife's dress. The relationship between we and my mother became more and more no friendly. Now we live alone. We call on my mother one or two times a week. The relationship changed for the better.

24

Communist Party Members

MARY ANN

AT EVERY STAGE OF the education system, Chinese people are aware of the Communist Party. In elementary school, children join the Young Pioneers, who imitate grown-up party members. One time Fran and I came across a group of Young Pioneers, with colorful red scarves around their necks, cheerfully making *jiaozi* on the sandy shores of the Tuo River in Luzhou. They could have been Boy Scouts and Girl Scouts. I wondered what the difference was really; all three organizations strive to engage young people in acts of patriotism and instill love for their country. Teenagers could join the Communist Youth League, which took an active role on college campuses. At age 18, a person could apply to join the party, though people were commonly accepted in their 20s. When adults joined the party, a very small percentage of their salary went to the party.

In the early 1980s, the Chinese Communist Party was lacking young people. Whereas about a quarter of all party members—26.6 percent—had been 25 years and younger in 1950, right after the Communist Revolution, by 1983 only 3.36 percent of party members were in that age bracket.[1]

The extent to which college students who joined the party were really loyal to its goals and ideals was uncertain. In a survey of students at eighteen Shanghai universities in 1988, participants responded to the question: "Some of your friends have joined the party, others are striving to do so.

1. Rosen, "The Impact of Reform Policies," 293.

106

What is your observation and understanding of this?" Only 4 percent of respondents answered, "They believe in Communism and want to make a contribution." Fifty-nine percent of respondents said, "In reality they want a 'party card' they can use as capital to receive future benefits."[2] Although the survey findings published by Chinese and Western academics reflected practices and attitudes of young people in large east coast cities, not in places in the interior of the country like Luzhou, it's likely that only a minority of our students who were still in their 20s were Communist Party members.

༄༅

I played a mental game in Luzhou: Identifying Party Members. The idea of party membership was novel and intriguing for an American. I'd heard a lot of propaganda about Communism and Communists while growing up in the United States during the Cold War, but before I went to China, I hadn't met anyone who professed to be a Communist. When I went to the movies as a teenager, the "good guys" were the Americans and the "bad guys" were the Russians—or Communists. We heard a lot more about the Russians than about the Chinese people in the 1960s and 1970s. I recall how James Bond was featured in movies outsmarting Russian Communist spies.

In China, a number of my teaching colleagues were probably Communists, and I had been programmed to be suspicious. The Chinese people were aware of Westerners' biases against Communists, so people did not go out of their way to tell us they were party members. I usually found out who the party members were from those who had deliberately decided *not* to join the party. The people who resisted joining the party expressed resentment about the reality that being a party member translated into privilege. Party members seemed to get plum jobs, promotions, and opportunities for study.

When I asked Teacher Lin whether most of the leaders of Luzhou Medical College were party members, he nodded emphatically and said, "Sure." He added, "They see it as a way to serve their country."

I speculated about who some of the party members among my students were based on their attitude toward attending Thursday afternoon political study sessions. I understood that everyone employed by educational

2. Zhao Yicheng, "*Jiazhide chongtu*" ("Value Conflict"), *Weidinggao*, 1988, quoted in Rosen, "The Impact of Reform Policies," 295.

institutions all across China attended political meetings one afternoon per week. They would discuss certain policies or issues, such as the problem of "bourgeois liberalization." I certainly hoped that in their discussions, these leaders didn't frequently mention Fran and me as possible vessels for spreading "decadent" Western culture.

Party members met at least twice a week. When I asked one middle-aged woman why she hadn't joined the party, she said, "One political meeting a week is enough!" Another person's explanation for not joining the party was simply "I'm not a Communist. I don't care."

Students and employees at Luzhou Medical College were organized into work units, and the Communist Party members in these work units kept close tabs on everyone else. Some of our students who weren't party members said they would groan and beg the class monitor or head of the work unit to cancel the Thursday meeting. They proposed alternative activities, such as reading and discussing articles from the *China Daily*, which were published in English. Sometimes if Luzhou Medical College hosted a special lecture, such as from a visiting doctor, our students would sign in at the political meeting and then skip out to attend the lecture.

Some women told me they tried to make the best use of the time they were required to spend in political meetings by knitting. I didn't ask these women directly whether they were party members, but I suspect they were not. I don't think a party member would knit, because other party members might criticize them for not being as engaged as possible.

Party members tended to be conscientious students and tried to give the impression of having good habits, such as doing one's job well and taking care of one's health. (Smoking didn't count.) Many party members seemed to feel responsible for providing an outward model of exemplary living, as a religious leader may do for an assembly of worshippers.

We learned to detect party ideologies of our students by perspectives that we heard repeatedly or that students would include in compositions. For instance, they wrote that the Chinese government had invested a lot of effort and money into "developing" Tibet, whereas Tibetans felt their country was occupied by China. Students also talked about Deng Xiaoping's open-door policy and the "four modernizations."

One of our students in our first intensive English class fit the mold of a party loyalist. Now the website of Southwest Medical University—formerly Luzhou Medical College—says she is the vice secretary of the Party Committee. That's a high-level party and administrative position.

Among our diligent students were also some students who resisted becoming Communist Party members. Their employers and superiors put tremendous pressure on them to join the party, so if they chose not to join, they were sometimes nonconformists in other ways. Our students who stood out in their desire to read and to understand us and bridge cultural gaps tended not to be Communist Party members though there were also exceptions to this pattern.

25

The Student Storyteller

MARY ANN

WE APPRECIATED ONE COMMUNIST Party member in the intensive English program during our third semester who was very open to writing and talking about his life experiences. Yan Jian was on the short list of people who seemed internally driven to help us understand China authentically. His storytelling started with a composition about how he hadn't wanted to become a doctor.

> When I learned the news that I should be a doctor, I was disappointed. In the afternoon of March 18, 1978, I was going to visit my brother who worked in a factory. While I was riding a bicycle past the Ming River bridge, I met him. At that time, I was surprised at his coming back. He told me: "I have received the information that you have been admitted into Luzhou Medical College as a college student." Oh, how disappointed I was! Though I was working in the countryside and I was looking forward to the day when I could study in a college, Luzhou Medical College could not satisfy me because it was very small and the quality of education was not so good. Furthermore, I was unwilling to be a doctor. So I said, "Let's go home and discuss whether or not I should go to the college."

Yan Jian was from Yibin (about a four-hour bus trip from Luzhou), where we had gone to see the stone forest, and he was the thirteenth of fifteen children in his family. However, only six of the children, four girls and two boys, had survived. According to Yan Jian, two months after his mother had given birth to one of his siblings, she had slipped with a pot of boiling water and burned her leg. She was in bed for half a year, and the newborn was given to relatives for care. In 1987, Yan Jian's father was 80 years old. His mother had already died. Yan Jian was 32 when he was our student. Because he got an education, he fared better than some of his siblings. His brother was a farmer.

∽♀↷

Memories of the Cultural Revolution were still fresh in Yan Jian's mind. He said that when different factions were fighting during the Cultural Revolution, his mother took young people into their home. One night, thirty people were staying in his home. Once he stated, "We are ashamed about the Cultural Revolution." I thought he was trying to say that, in looking back, people were embarrassed about their participation in the harmful groupthink that occurred.

Yan Jian was one of the few people who admitted to us a connection he had to someone who was religious. He said he had a cousin who was a monk in Kunming. He told us he himself had been really interested in Buddhism until he'd become a Communist Party member. Then, he said, he'd had to give up his interest.

From his perspective, some of the "superstitions" from Old China had not been done away with. He wrote:

> The wedding in China today is modern, but some old-fashioned superstitions still remain. For example, the bride can not go to her new house on foot on her wedding day. It means that her husband maybe does not love her, if she herself has to decide to go to her husband's home. She would be ignored. Also, she never goes into the wedding room unless her mother-in-law gives her a gift, usually a little money packed in a red paper. With that the mother shows her concern to the bride. Besides, we all know that the bride should not sweep the floor because she knows she's a noble girl and she would be regarded as a worthless worker if she did so.

When we taught Yan Jian, he had been working at Luzhou Medical College for four years. He said he wasn't using his training in his particular field. It seemed very common that the college didn't fully tap the talents of young people; they often weren't put in responsible positions. In addition, they didn't have much choice for their career path. For example, another student we taught for two semesters said he had wanted to be a researcher. He was instead assigned to be a teacher in the chemistry department at Luzhou Medical College. He had been promised that after working for the college for two years, he would have a chance to take entrance exams for graduate school. "The leader broke his promise," he said.

In addition to talking about his career, Yan Jian shared about people's day-to-day lives. Many people were striving to acquire appliances that included a washing machine, television, and refrigerator. Our students joked that up-to-date appliances were the "modernizations" that Chinese people were focused on, rather than the official four modernizations. Yan Jian wrote about how he didn't expect to acquire a refrigerator any time soon:

> Owning a refrigerator will be expensive inspite of more and more families having an ice-box. First, you have to pay about one thousand *yuan* to buy a new refrigerator. According to my salary one hundred each month, subtracting the necessary expense, I can only save thirty *yuan* each month. So it will need forty months for me to deposit one thousand. Furthermore, the main problem is the charge of electricity. You have to pay 22 *yuan* each day and 6.6 *yuan* each month. Many people said, "I can offer one thousand *yuan* to buy a refrigerator, but I'm unable to have enough money to pay on the charge of electricity." So, refrigerator has not been very popular by now.

Our students tended to put a positive spin on the events in their lives when sharing with us, particularly if they were Communist Party members. That wasn't the case with Yan Jian. He was a party member who didn't always adhere to the party line.

26

The Character
of the Chinese Language

FRAN

ONE DAY, ALMOST EIGHTEEN months after we arrived in Luzhou, we hung
out in the apartment of a young English teacher for seven and a half hours.
The affair involved a lot of people cooking and talking. For about an hour
of that time, we chatted in Chinese about food with one of the middle-aged
women who was helping to cook a slew of Sichuan dishes: pork and peanuts, bamboo shoot soup, *mala* beef, salad, and fish. We weren't up to the
competency of the cooks in the kitchen, so we watched and conversed with
them. When a young man was getting ready to cut off the head of a catfish
with a knife on the balcony of the apartment, the fish leaped off the balcony
and fell to the ground six floors below! The young man ran downstairs to
rescue the main dish.

It had taken us many months to get to the point at which we could
speak Chinese for an hour about an everyday topic. Although our language
process was usually painstaking, that day we returned home without the
usual frustration, satisfied with ourselves for once.

൭൭

Prior to living in Luzhou, we didn't consider extensive Chinese language study necessary before working as English teachers there. However,

although we railed a lot against the restrictions on our social interaction in Luzhou, we must admit our lack of fluency in the Chinese language limited our ability to interact with Chinese people nearly as much as any restrictions on social interactions did.

\ঙঠ\

Both of us experienced periods in which we were motivated to learn Chinese, but then also plenty of times of discouragement because it was so hard. We focused on learning *putonghua*, Mandarin, the language taught in the education system and used publicly across China. However, everyone around us spoke the Sichuan dialect in everyday life, which had different vocabulary and expressions than standard Chinese. Mary Ann felt that learning Chinese even surpassed the challenge of learning calculus in high school, which had not gone well for her. I could not think of any learning experience that was more intense.

We had both been motivated to pick up some basic *putonghua* before coming to China. I enrolled in a short-term class for two months through the YWCA in Boston where I was teaching junior high school students. The Chinese teacher was energetic and a firm believer in the immersion method, a conversational approach that I appreciated. Even though I emerged from each class session with a mild headache, I did learn some essential phrases like *Ni hao* (Hello), *Wode mingzi shi Fran* (My name is Fran), and *Cesuo zai nar* (Where is the bathroom?). Later, on my way out of China, I thought, "It is crazy to be here for two years and not know the language. If I had it to do over, I'd know the language up and down first."

In Mary Ann's case, she had received a brief but strong start in Chinese with a teacher from Beijing. CEE paid for these lessons at a language institute in Manhattan where Mary Ann was living and working prior to teaching in China. During the semester when she was a teacher in Chengdu, Mary Ann had started to make a couple of friends who didn't speak English, and there she had the freedom to hang out with people her own age. She knew a few basic phrases in Chinese by the time she moved to Luzhou.

The fact that Mary Ann had been in China a half year longer than I and knew a little more Chinese than I did created a dynamic such that if we two were chatting with people in Chinese, Mary Ann was inclined to speak for me. One time after we had been conversing with the neighbors, and

Mary Ann had been responding to all the questions, I got angry and lashed out. That was rare for me, but Mary Ann realized at that moment that we two were on an uneven playing field and that she needed to let me speak for myself and have a chance to try out the language.

At some point, we requested private language lessons, which we paid for out of our allowance. It took a while for the school to set up these lessons. In the meantime, although we worked in English, we made it a point to exchange pleasantries in Chinese with the neighbors. We learned numbers and words like *meimei* (little sister) and *didi* (little brother) from them. Although we had tried soliciting our first interpreter, Teacher Luo, to give us Chinese lessons, those lessons had soon petered out. It wasn't her job.

Well into our second semester of teaching, we were finally assigned a Chinese-language teacher who spoke excellent standard Chinese. Ma Jing was 23 and an opinionated female Communist Party member with little sense of humor. She was an exacting teacher, and we often left our session feeling dumb as oxen.

The week's lesson consisted of some conversation, but actually contained quite a lot of memorization of characters. Some of the characters had up to twenty-four strokes that needed to be completed in a certain order. The torture of the hour was taking dictation—writing down in characters the words our tutor uttered. I was a visual learner and so did not despise this practice as much as Mary Ann did; she saw learning characters as a diversion from the more important task of learning how to converse in Chinese.

The intensity of memorization taxed the minds of us young Americans who were used to more creative, problem-solving learning; our memory muscle was rather weak. We could understand now the ability of Chinese children to memorize. Watching them painstakingly write characters out with their grandparents on park tables everywhere made us aware of an area of brain development American children were missing out on. We could also see how the difficulty of learning Chinese characters had, in ancient China, been a means of separating the elite scholars from the masses. The elitists were literate because they had the time to devote to studying characters.

In any case, our teacher put up with our clumsy use of the language, and we with her no-nonsense style. Only one time did our instructor break out of her reserve—one of us said something in Chinese that was clearly not what was intended. She snorted and then left the room abruptly. We could hear her laughter from outside, and it took her quite a while to compose herself and come back in; if we only knew what had been said! She never told us.

Outside of study hours, we found it somewhat bothersome that our language teacher would show up at our door and want to go out on the town with us to shop. On the steep walk down the mountain into town, Ma Jing adopted the Chinese habit of tucking our arms under hers in a chummy fashion. This sort of clinging did not arise from true affection, like that we experienced with Zhang Dongni, but rather seemed to be a calculated move intended to show her connection to the American teachers and improve her status. We did, however, appreciate that these outings gave us a chance to have an immersion experience, since Ma Jing did not speak any English.

One evening after Mary Ann had returned to the United States, my new fellow teachers and I went to a party that Teacher Ma insisted we attend. (After our third effort to decline, we gave in.) It was as we had feared: we were placed in a seat of honor, which meant we were expected to greet each guest in Chinese as he or she came in. We also had to give a "performance," which ended up being our go-to option of a poor rendition of Peter, Paul, and Mary's "If I Had a Hammer." After that uncomfortable evening, one of my colleagues quit Chinese study altogether, opting for "self-study." Oh, how I envied that bold move.

౪౾

In the two summers between our teaching semesters, all the CEE English teachers met to study Chinese for several weeks. The first summer, Mary Ann and I studied with the teacher group at Nanjing Teachers College on the east coast of China. Nanjing, a midsize, relatively modern city with plenty of foreign tourists, was a welcome change from Luzhou.

Nanjing was also a city rich in historic sites. It was the final resting place of the famous Sun Yat-sen, the provisional first president of the Republic of China and founder of the Kuomintang Nationalist Party. It was also, unfortunately, the site of the Rape of Nanjing perpetrated by Japanese soldiers in 1937. Moreover, it was the place of the Taiping Rebellion in the mid-1800s when a man named Hong Xiuquan, who thought he was

Christ's younger brother, led a peasant uprising that was supposed to bring about a "Heavenly Kingdom."[1]

Nanjing was also one of the many "furnaces" in China, along with Chongqing and Wuhan, as people loved to tell us. It had high humidity and soaring temperatures that forced the locals to put mats out on the sidewalk to seek a cooler place to sleep. People consumed abundant numbers of watermelons—huge piles of them were sold everywhere on the streets.

Our accommodations were sparse but clean dorm rooms at the college. The food was good and the classrooms were grand. They were in the main reception hall of a beautiful dark-wood, traditional-style building. Since Mary Ann and I had learned more Chinese than some, we were put in the advanced group, alongside a ridiculously fast learner, our friend Ann Martin. While some of us were struggling to say sentences like "I enjoy traveling around China," Ann was putting together constructions like "The child pushed his homemade toy across the room to his adoring mother." But we could not hate her, since she was the one who always kept us laughing, encouraging us all to speak Chinese outside of class in an American Southern drawl—"*Niiii de shenti, hen haooooo*"—and dubbing our exercise teacher Mr. Shenti Hen Hao (Mr. Body Very Good).

As with our studies in Luzhou, the worst part was the dictation. Our teacher pointed out that my handwriting was *bu hao kan* (not beautiful), which was also true of my handwriting in English. On the positive side, the teacher felt that my writing skills in Chinese were strong. I found it intriguing that writing abilities in the English language carried over to Chinese. By the end of the summer, I could boast that I was able to recognize and write one thousand characters. What good that did me, I am not sure, since now I can scarcely remember ten, but that was the accomplishment of the summer.

Mary Ann, meanwhile, struggled mightily with learning characters. At the same time, she started showing off by writing some of the characters she did learn in letters to people in the United States. She liked to sign off with the characters for *man zou* (Walk slowly), one of her favorite Chinese expressions. People would say it as a way to wish guests well when they were leaving and starting out on the path toward home.

Mary Ann and I ultimately realized that it was not so much the intensive language training in the classroom as the traveling during semester breaks that created some of the best immersion experiences for learning

1. Reilly, *The Taiping Heavenly Kingdom*.

Chinese. The hours we spent on buses and trains seated right next to Chinese people of all walks of life gave us a chance to practice the language. People were curious and asked us questions. There was one speech in Chinese that Mary Ann would say over and over; she was quite proud of it and can still deliver it today: "My name is Mary Ann. I'm American. I teach English. I teach at Luzhou Medical College. It's located on the Chang Jiang (Yangtze River)." After we had each been in the country for more than a year, we realized we would never be fluent in Chinese, but we were thrilled that we knew enough Chinese to handle travel logistics.

My great triumph occurred on my final trip out of China when, at a local restaurant that tried to charge double since I was a foreigner (a common practice), I was able to argue with the woman in Chinese! I walked away so proud; my limited Chinese was useful for something, if only to preserve my dignity and express my outrage at being viewed only as deep pockets.

What also happened, as often does when one learns another language, is that I adopted a different persona. I reflected that Fu Lang Xi Si, the Chinese name for Frances, signaled a shift in who I was. That person often argued vociferously in the market over a few extra cents for vegetables and was bold in making banquet toasts and pronouncements about Western culture to a packed hall of interested listeners. Sometimes, indeed, it felt like playacting. At times my alternate personality made me braver and allowed me a deeper look into the Chinese person I was speaking with; at other times, it made me feel alienated from my true self, in yet another realm of isolation. Like almost anything in China, language learning ended up as a study in contrasts.

27

The Rules Loosen Up a Tad

Mary Ann

We picnic with fellow Luzhou Medical College English teachers.

OUT OF THE BLUE, it seemed as if the *waiban* was getting lax. During our second April in Luzhou, the Chinese English teachers planned a picnic that included us, and no one from the *waiban* went along, which was a first for a day trip. We traveled to a local spot called Phoenix Lake, named after what is the most common Chinese mythological creature aside from the dragon.

We were all appropriately dressed for a typical chilly, damp day in Sichuan with lots of layers, including outer jackets and sweaters.

For a snack, we chewed on fresh sugarcane stalks. We tried out the pedal boats on the lake, four people to a boat. Then the teachers spread picnic food out on a cloth on the ground amid a stand of trees. A cluster of people stood not too far from us, staring at Fran and me, but we all ignored them. We teachers squatted around, drinking beer and eating cold meat dishes, spitting the bones out on the ground. The men smoked.

We played games. Frisbee was our contribution because someone had sent us a Frisbee from the United States. We also played Chinese checkers (with marbles) and cards. No one went out of their way to make us feel as if we were different from anyone else, except that the English teachers spoke English with Fran and me. They spoke the Sichuan dialect among themselves.

A few months later, on a warm afternoon in April, students from our third intensive English class in Luzhou planned an outing on the sandy shores of the Tuo River, which runs into the Yangtze River. The Tuo River is smaller and more scenic than the Yangtze. Its shallow waters by the shores make wading possible.

Once again, the older male *waiban* officials decided not to accompany us. Like our first class of students, this class had a lot of students in their 20s, as well as a few middle-aged people. Our students included members of the Communist Party who likely later gave a full report on our activity. And Zhang Dongni, our interpreter who worked for the *waiban*, came along. She had our trust. Because it was only our class of students there, and no veteran cadres, we felt light and free.

What was wonderful was that we hung out with our students by the river for hours, and people seemed to relax and be their authentic selves. We played Frisbee football, rolled up our pants and waded in the river, relaxed on a cloth spread out on the sand, played music loudly, played cards, and talked. Students always seemed to make themselves more vulnerable in their storytelling if we were outside of class—and also away from the ears of the *waiban*. Two students brought a bit of history into the conversation:

"Before Liberation, my uncle had two wives. After 1949, one of them separated and moved to another town and got married again," said Yan Jian, the student who had a flair for telling stories in compositions.

We relax by the Tuo River with our third intensive English class.

"Your family must be rich. Maybe your grandfather was a landlord," responded a young woman.

"No. My grandfather was a capitalist. Before Liberation, my family was rich, but after Liberation, we were very poor. Anyhow, I love the Communist Party."

Yan Jian waded into the river water, caught a crayfish, and showed it around to everyone. We watched wooden junks go by on the river. We sometimes saw someone cooking in the hull of the boat or a boy urinating off of the deck. Sometimes rowers on junks sang folk songs. I was inspired by the rivers in Luzhou and eventually wrote a haiku about the mighty Yangtze River, or Chang Jiang, in Chinese.

> A lone junk floats down
> the Chang River, ignoring
> morning dragon breath.

With our class of students, we walked to an outdoor restaurant and had a meal together. The owner of the restaurant worked in one of Luzhou's many wine factories. He was also an artist. He showed us beautiful brush paintings in his home, which was next to the restaurant. They were created in the mountain-river style. Tired and happy, our students, Fran, and I took a public bus back to school.

The fact that the *waiban* leaders had trusted us enough to let us spend hours with our students doing casual activities boosted our morale. Maybe the school officials were starting to "get us" just a bit. It really didn't take much to make us feel over the moon.

ॐ

At the end of May, Fran and I had another wonderful outing without any *waiban* accompanying us. One of our students, Gao Xin, hosted us for a day trip to an active Buddhist temple on Fangshan Mountain. Gao Xin was a student in his 40s who worked at a nearby chemical research institute and was a member of the intensive English class.

By local bus, the trip to the starting point took about a half hour. Then it was time for a strenuous hike up Fangshan Mountain to the temple. Gao Xin was a thoughtful host. He carried a watermelon up to the top of the mountain and split it open with a knife for refreshment.

I'd probably been to a dozen temples in China, but this one was the most interesting. We learned that the oldest section of the temple had been built in the Tang Dynasty (618–907). The rest was built in the Qing Dynasty, which lasted until 1911.

As was true of churches, temples had been closed during the Cultural Revolution and became active again only in 1978. Our students' compositions indicated that some families had maintained or revived Buddhist practices, such as burning money for the dead. One student wrote:

> Next Sunday we'll go to sweep my father's in law tomb. It's a Chinese traditional custom: In Chin Min days (before or after April 5) every year, each family will go to his older generation's tomb to express their mourning—named "sweeping tomb." First, in the front of the tombstone, we'll put some pork and a cup of wine. Then burn many pieces of "paper money," which are sent to the dead to use in the other world. The more pieces of money we burn, the richer the dead will become. Finally, we'll kowtow and pray to him to bless us. Meanwhile we'll repair the tomb.

At the temple on Fangshan Mountain, we observed a worship service with eight monks. They chanted, hit a bell-like instrument with a hammer, sang, and clanged cymbals. Two people kowtowed on the floor cushions in front of a shrine. For a small admission fee, the monks showed us treasures of the temple: a bead with a Buddha carved on it, a fan, and a fossil of a sword.

We talked with a monk who said he was from the neighboring province, Guizhou. He had lived at the temple for thirty-eight years. He showed us a photo of himself with some other monks that had been taken in 1964 by an old gate of the temple. The gate wasn't standing anymore; I imagined it had been destroyed during the Cultural Revolution.

The same monk took us out to the burial grounds for monks. I asked him if he wanted to stand with us for a photo to be taken. He refused. But after Fran and I posed alone for a photo, he said, "If we are walking, I will be in your picture." He gave us a tour of the tombs, and I snapped a photo.

We took in rural scenes. Peasants were laying out grain to dry that had already been used for making wine. We saw several Buddha statues, which had clearly received visitors, set up along the road in the countryside. Cans stood near the Buddhas that held partly burned incense.

How was it possible that the *waiban* had permitted a lone student to take Fran and me on an outing for almost a whole day? The truth was that they did not find out about the trip until after the fact. Gao Xin told us, with frustration in his voice, that college leaders had reprimanded him when they learned about the trip. However, he also waved off the criticism. Because Gao Xin was employed by an entity other than Luzhou Medical College, he was a member of a work unit outside the college. I hope I am right in thinking that college leaders didn't have the power to make any trouble for him.

༄༅༅

Fran and I held an end-of-the-term tea party for our third class of intensive English students. We served tea, peaches, and brownies we had baked in a recently purchased toaster oven. Everyone seemed to relax, and Fran and I did not feel as if we were orchestrating everything for once. It seemed that the students asked whatever questions came to mind, and we did the same. They asked:

"Are most Americans really self-centered?"

"What are you most afraid of in the United States?"

"Do Americans have drinking games?"

We asked: "What do you like best about China?" Some of the answers were job security, a sense of safety, history, and peacefulness.

Several students and I got into a discussion about whether people's knowledge of their country's history speeds up or impedes progress. Another student told me his story about how he hadn't been admitted to a music college in 1979, even though he had passed the entrance exam, because his family was "counterrevolutionary." I felt honored that he had trusted me with his story.

The biggest event of the evening, besides the frank talk, was the distribution of awards. Fran and I had made up silly but truthful awards for each of the thirty or so students whom we jointly taught, noting their special characteristics. We wrote out imitation certificates, pasted on tinfoil seals, and signed our names. I guess they were a hit because the awards flattered students as individuals, and the idea was fresh to them.

The awards included ones for the most humorous student, the most likely to answer questions in class, the person most knowledgeable about Chinese traditions, the best musician, the best dictionary user (for a student who was always debating the pronunciation or meaning of words with me, with evidence from his dictionary), the most modern, and the most likely to be late to class. The students laughed and clapped for each person.

A wonderful time with students in our tearoom

28

Teacher Lin Leaves Us Perplexed

MARY ANN

BESIDES ZHANG DONGNI, THE Chinese person we spent the most time with in Luzhou was Teacher Lin. He considered it part of his job to keep us entertained. It seemed he truly wanted us to have a favorable impression of China—and of Luzhou in particular.

Teacher Lin had been the first person on campus to invite us to his home for a meal, a memorable and lavish feast. His wife had cooked and served gourmet foods that had included duck, fungus soup, pickled vegetables, pork dumplings, and a dessert of sweet, glutinous rice balls in a syrup.

That evening Teacher Lin told us he had previously been a teacher at Sichuan Normal University, the same teachers' university where I had taught for a semester before moving to Luzhou. He said he had volunteered to transfer from Chengdu to Luzhou, which was unusual because many Chinese people believed the benefits of living in a larger city were greater than those of living in a small city like Luzhou. Most people viewed a move from a big city to a small one as a demotion. Teacher Lin said he had liked the medical college and had felt he could be of use there. He was jovial and charismatic, and I could see how he had worked his way up into the administration, first in the English department and then in the *waiban*.

Teacher Lin surprised us on several occasions. One such time was when he quoted a couple of Bible verses, and that in the presence of two other cadres. Fran and I looked at each other, amazed that a Communist Party leader was quoting scripture. At another time, he informed us that he had attended the local church near his campus in Ohio a few times. Had that been simply out of curiosity, we wondered, or had he found something there that appealed to him? One thing we felt for sure: he intentionally referred to the Bible and his church visit to help us be more comfortable with him, to trust him.

Teacher Lin spent a lot of energy and time taking Fran and me on outings on weekends. He had good ideas for field trips; we couldn't have come up with them on our own. Luzhou wasn't included in the 1984 Lonely Planet guidebook for China, the backpacker's Bible.

On the outings, Teacher Lin would engage in lively conversation with us. Once he took us to Zigong to see dinosaur bones that had been recently uncovered and were displayed in a brand-new museum. On that trip he explained to us opportunities that would be available for our students if they could pass standardized English tests. Teacher Lin told us the World Health Organization had promised it would send five people from Luzhou abroad to study if they could pass the tests. Previously, we had thought it was a pipe dream that medical professionals from an institution lacking prestige in China, such as Luzhou Medical College, would be given the privilege of studying abroad. The only person we knew in Luzhou who had gone abroad for graduate school was Teacher Lin.

Another time, Teacher Lin took us to a government-run orchard where we bought dozens of large, sweet tangerines. On that day, he told stories about when he worked as an interpreter for negotiation sessions for the joint project between Americans and the Luzhou Chemical Company in the 1970s. Teacher Lin said the foreigners didn't think the project was moving along fast enough. I've since learned the construction project came out of a multimillion-dollar contract China made with the M. W. Kellogg Company to build eight synthetic fertilizer plants in China.[1] As a result, American and Dutch technicians lived in Luzhou in 1974 and 1975 (and maybe longer), before the end of the Cultural Revolution, housed in a three-story guesthouse.[2]

At one point in our conversation, Teacher Lin offered a judgment about foreigners. He said, "We think Westerners are rather selfish, but there are a few really, really good people who are unusual and care about others."

I took this statement to refer to the Americans whom Teacher Lin had met at the fertilizer plant as well as the ones he had encountered during

1. Wilcke, "Kellogg," para. 2.
2. Zhu, "Secret Trails," 168–9.

his two years of studying at Ohio State University. I wondered: In which category did Teacher Lin put Fran and me? Did he think we were selfish, or did he think we cared about people?

Though we were often charmed by Teacher Lin, we got the sense that he did what he could to keep us from forming personal relationships with Chinese people. I couldn't let go of my frustration that Fran and I weren't permitted to visit the homes of students, and it bothered me that Teacher Lin would not acknowledge to us that this was the policy. One time, I pressed him and other *waiban* officials on the issue; when they didn't admit that the restriction existed, I lost control of my emotions. I cried and left the room. Unfortunately, my outburst put Fran in a difficult spot, because I left her in the room to deal with the officials. My outburst wasn't effective in changing the situation, but it was therapeutic. I reflected in writing that "the whole affair taught me that confrontation is difficult in Chinese society. I don't feel any bitterness toward the officials in the *waiban*—they've done everything for us. I do think, though, that it doesn't hurt to state our differences now and then. We aren't Chinese people and we can't follow the direction of the Party like the people do here."

৩৩৶

Just before I ended my stay in Luzhou, at a social event in a downtown apartment (the occasion where the catfish leaped off a balcony), Teacher Lin suggested that he had miscalculated how American teachers—of course, that meant Fran and I—would adjust to living in Luzhou. I speculate that when Teacher Lin and other college leaders had decided to invite us to live in Luzhou, initially a "closed city," they hadn't anticipated how we and our Chinese students would resist their efforts to escort us everywhere except the dining hall and the classroom. Did they really think they could confine us to a few physical spaces on campus and control what we said and with whom we spoke?

The social gathering was in a new high-rise apartment building off campus in Luzhou city, one that represented how the city's landscape was quickly being modernized.

"Luzhou has changed a lot physically and otherwise since Fran and I arrived," I said.

"Yes. It's become less confined," Teacher Lin remarked. "I had thought maybe you religious people wouldn't mind the confinement." And his tone said: "You have minded it!"

"We aren't used to it," I quickly responded.

Teacher Lin and I often sparred lightly in conversation. I thought he was competent, and I secretly predicted that he might become president of Luzhou Medical College someday. I think he also viewed Fran and me as competent—he never asked for any adjustments in our teaching. He could have asked us to focus our curriculum on preparing students for standardized English tests, but he didn't. I think Teacher Lin was surprised by how blunt I was sometimes, but he also seemed to respect it and often responded to my direct comments with equally blunt remarks.

Looking back, I recognize that my younger self didn't appreciate all the pressures Teacher Lin faced to make sure foreign teachers didn't embarrass him or the college. I had only a superficial understanding of the political whiplash the Chinese people had experienced with abrupt changes in the government's political goals. I also was too quick to attribute all roadblocks in cross-cultural relationships to the fact that the society was governed by one political party—the Communist Party, which I viewed as having conditioned Chinese people for decades to be suspicious of foreigners. The fact was that distrust of foreigners was a long thread in Chinese history. It hadn't started with the 1949 Communist Revolution.

❧

As I prepared to leave Luzhou and return to the United States, I felt a sense of satisfaction that Teacher Lin, other college leaders, and students were happy with our teaching. Mennonite and Chinese cultures share the value of diligence, and the medical college leaders took note of our "hard work."

But I struggled to evaluate how well I'd succeeded at making meaningful connections with Chinese people, and I blamed Teacher Lin for having constructed obstacles. I felt affection and admiration—even love—for students and colleagues on campus. I'd met some thinkers who had really humbled me. They had told me about challenges that they faced to continue to think freely. They said they had to keep some ideas to themselves, or maybe express them only to close friends. Otherwise, they might risk offending someone and hampering their chances for study or promotion. I appreciated my students' warmth toward us and their efforts to tell us the truth. I appreciated their curiosity about our country and other countries. We'd had many moments of authenticity, understanding, and laughter. At the same time, it seemed these moments had been fleeting. One could say I'd experienced friendship in the aggregate more than personally with Chinese people in Luzhou. It took me decades to recognize how precious even that kind of friendship is.

ॳ৶

In a gesture of farewell, the *waiban* officials presented me (and later they did the same for Fran) with a video chronicling our time there, including our day trips out to orchards, class times, and tea times, complete with running comments by Teacher Lin: "Why is Miss Martens smiling?" "Miss Zehr is having a vivid conversation with her student." It must have taken him a very long time to narrate the video.

After I'd left China, I occasionally received a card from the Luzhou Medical College *waiban*. I received a Christmas card signed by Zhang Dongni and Teacher Lin in December 1988. "We still remember the good times we shared in Luzhou, China," the card said.

I received another card from the medical college's *waiban* dated September 10, 1989, soon after the events in Tiananmen Square. The card said "Chinese Teacher's Day." It said: "Warm Greetings. You and your hard work are remembered. Thank you CEE Teacher."

29

School Restrictions and Student Kindness

FRAN

IN THE LAST SEMESTER of my time in Luzhou, I learned to adjust to my new teaching companions—a bouncy American named Kim with amusing metaphorical speech and a serious-minded Canadian named Winnie. As time went by, I noticed that China continued to have more and more goods available in the market: brown sugar, whole grain wheat, canned tomatoes. We decided to add to our company a blue budgie we found in the market. That turned out to be a good choice, since parents came around to show their children the bird, which created a better sense of community with our neighbors.

One day, in November 1987, I had an experience in the market that I will never forget. Winnie was accompanying me into town to the fruit market, and we suddenly came upon a group of four Tibetan men. They had spread out their woolen blankets on the sidewalk and placed upon them animal skulls and herbs of every kind to sell for medicinal and fertility/virility purposes and who knows what else. Winnie stopped to take a picture, and the apparent leader of the group said we couldn't, not unless she made a bargain with him to give him a copy. When he said he would be in town for the next three months, she agreed and took the picture, planning to take the film down to the new local Kodak photo shop to develop, a process that took several days.

A few days later, there was loud banging on our door. The Tibetan men were there in the moonlight, outside our lower balcony, daggers glistening by their sides, and drunk. Some wore animal-skin hats and long, drab robes. They said they were leaving town the next day and demanded their picture! They were none too happy when Winnie said it was not ready. We stood there nervously, wondering what to do and where campus security was when we really needed them.

Then our next-door neighbor showed up and helped translate, though she was rather frightened too. Finally, we made the men understand that we were not tricking them and that we did not in fact have the pictures yet, that they were being developed at the shop. We asked them to write down their addresses and said we would send them the photos. After much debate, they agreed. The leader said he would write his mama's address and made motions of crying—his mother from his hometown in Qinghai Province was missing him. It was so strange, this big guy in a felt derby hat, a dagger by his side, saying his mommy was crying for him!

Once the agreement had been made, the Tibetans became very polite. We gave them tangerines, and they bowed and accepted them. Then they left and we sighed with relief, dropping into our chairs in the sitting room and trying to process what had just happened.

Strangely enough, three days later we saw two of them in the marketplace. They looked embarrassed and said their transportation had broken down so they were staying longer. The odd thing is, I do not remember whether we ever sent the photos in the end.

Tibetan traders display their wares in Luzhou.

Some things in Luzhou were not new, however. The restrictions on our friendships with Chinese students and staff on campus continued—even after brief periods when things seemed to be easing up. One of these events happened just before I left Luzhou for good. We were trying to plan a social weekend. For a Friday night event, we invited some of our students over to cook hot pot, a Sichuan specialty. Then students canceled on us suddenly—they told us they were busy. Then for the next night, we had invited the English teachers over for an early Christmas party. But when Saturday night came, there was a major mix-up, and in the end, only three out of nineteen showed up as "representatives of the group." The rest apparently had some sort of sudden "political meeting." We thought that sounded suspicious. We were greatly disappointed because we had made peppernuts (German Mennonite cookies) and had planned activities, songs, and a time of decorating our little Christmas tree that we had borrowed from the school's decorative display outside the cinema. We ended up doing none of the above. Instead, after the "representatives" left, we ran to the next building and dragged one of our students away from her apartment to come and help us eat the leftovers. We looked for more students, but they were all away at the campus movie or had gone home to their families in town. It was a real letdown and depressingly familiar. We never found out the real reason nobody showed up.

Despite the barriers the school put up between us and our students, both we and our students still somehow and persistently found a way to connect. One day I had an intriguing outing with a student from my previous year's class. We went to buy carp in the market. It was a disgusting day—drizzling, cold—and the muddy fish market echoed the mood of the weather. When a new fisherman would appear with a fresh basket of catch, he'd be swarmed, people tearing at the lids of the baskets, until he would lose his temper and deliberately set up shop very slowly. After a lot of bartering, we got two carp for a total of 6 *yuan* (about two dollars). Then we trooped off to buy other ingredients and came back to our apartment to make two kinds of fish—fried, flayed fish and sweet-and-sour fish. The upshot is that I cleaned and scaled my first fish ever! We were joined by a few other former students and relished the delicious food.

In November, I got a visit from one last person, someone of great importance to me: my boyfriend, Ken. He had arranged a semester teaching assignment in China during my last semester with the hopes that we would get to see each other more often. The long tenure apart was wearing on both of us.

When at last Ken made the long flight from southern Africa—where he had been a teacher for three years—to Beijing, China, I met him at the airport. However, my elation soon turned to consternation. I had understood that he was to be teaching in a college in Guiyang City, about a five-hour train ride from Luzhou, in a neighboring province. He bounced off the plane, cheerfully declaring that his teaching assignment had been switched and that he now was going to be teaching at Northeast University of Technology in Liaoning Province. He had no idea where that was in China. I gasped. That university was in the far Northeast! I was teaching in the Southwest. We had ended up just about as far apart as possible. In those days in China, his being stationed in Liaoning Province was, in reality, no better than being stationed in Lesotho! I groaned, thinking of how it was nearly impossible to communicate by phone in China. And, of course, it was out of the question to visit each other since that would require a train trip of several days or an expensive flight.

Eventually, however, Ken did make it to Sichuan, to Luzhou Medical College. Students and faculty were all very pleased to see this elusive "boyfriend" who actually existed in the flesh. After hanging around Luzhou for several days, we took a break to go to the bigger and more modern city of Chengdu with its many restaurants, parks, museums, and colleges.

Ken in Sichuan, China, 1987.

It was in Chengdu that Ken and I got engaged. After knowing each other for eight years and dating for four of those, we figured it was time to make the decision. Thus, we made the call home to our parents. We went down to the Chengdu post office, waited in line to be called into a phone booth, called first my parents and then his, talking over a crackling phone line. We were elated . . . but not for long. Four days later, after intense conversations, we decided to break it off. Down again we trudged to the post office, waited again, called again. It was an excruciating time for both of us. (For the record, we did end up getting reengaged about six months later and married shortly thereafter.)

When it got closer to the time I was to leave Luzhou, I got a slew of unannounced visitors. Once, a group of students from the previous year's class came to see me. I felt glad they still remembered me and wanted to see me one more time before I left. On another occasion a kind, older student appeared at the door with a bagful of vegetables. "I just thought you didn't get a chance to go to town and buy food today, since it is raining," he explained.

Zhang Dongni and a factory worker friend made it a habit to come over to my apartment every Wednesday night to play Chinese checkers and eat popcorn with us teachers. As I was preparing to leave, I realized that these everyday moments with Chinese friends were what I was going to miss most.

Finally, the day came when I waved goodbye to those gathered to see me off and got on a train to head south to Guangzhou with several other CEE teachers. There I made my last visit to the Friendship Store, an expensive place for tourists that sold high-quality, handmade crafts such as embroidered wall hangings, silk scarves, and jade jewelry.

On our way back to the hotel with our acquired souvenirs, we got on a bus that was quite crowded. We had to stand, clutching our handbags with one hand and holding on to a strap from an overhead bar with the other. At the next stop, a bunch of people got on, and we were packed in tightly like sardines. We could hardly move. After a few stops, the crowd got off, and soon after, we got off too. Suddenly one of the teachers gave a cry of dismay. The front pocket of her jacket had been slit open and her money taken. The rest of us looked around and found that we had been robbed as well. Apparently, a gang of pickpockets had gotten on and off the bus together, jostling us in a way that we did not realize was intentional. I checked my backpack. Ah, my wallet was still there. But then, oh no! I discovered that the little book into which my Chinese friends—students, teachers, fellow travelers—had scribbled their addresses was missing. It seemed that the pickpockets had mistaken that for my wallet. It was a testament to the relationships that I had with my Chinese friends that, at that moment, I fervently wished the robbers had taken the wallet instead—my address book was the greater loss. Although I felt ready to leave China and return to the West, I had really wanted to stay in touch with my Chinese friends, and I already missed them.

PART III:
Beyond Luzhou
and Coming Full Circle

30

Tibet and the Wild West

Mary Ann

THE ULTIMATE, ABOVE-ALL DESTINATION for backpackers was Tibet, the independent country that the Chinese government occupied after the Communist Revolution in 1949. So when I completed my Luzhou teaching contract in June 1987, I sought adventure by heading there. Later, after reading my letters about the trip, Fran longed to go there too. However, that was not to be. Tibetan Buddhist monks marched with Tibetan flags in September 1987 as an affront to the Chinese government, so all foreign journalists and travelers were banned from the area. My friend Sherri Clark (a CEE teacher) and I managed to travel to Tibet just a couple of months before its status changed from "open" to "closed."

The train line that the Chinese government has built to Lhasa, the town in the heart of Tibet, didn't exist back then, so we took the train to the westernmost point possible, Golmud in Xinjiang province, and then we traveled by bus to Lhasa.

Before we got on the train to Golmud, though, we visited the terracotta soldiers in Xi'an. In these kinds of tourist spots, we encountered Chinese people with strong entrepreneurial—dare I say capitalist—tendencies. The poster at the booth where we bought tickets for transport to the site showed a spacious tour bus with large glass windows. Our actual transport was a regular city bus that had bad shocks and stuck windows.

The life-size terracotta soldiers were impressive for their representation of individual features—possibly mimicking the features of real people

139

from the past. One soldier was a shorty. I'm only an inch taller than five feet, so I could identify with him. Some soldiers looked youthful; others appeared to be elderly. Some stood straight; others slumped or had small hunchbacks. Some had mustaches; others lacked any facial hair. In addition to seeing the archeological wonder of the terracotta soldiers, Sherri and I enjoyed exploring the neighborhoods of Muslims. We dined on mutton and chili folded into pita-like bread with yogurt, as well as glutinous rice and bean paste made by Hui people, a minority group. The Hui men wore white caps, signaling their Islamic faith.

In a small souvenir shop at the Xi'an mosque, we witnessed a squabble between a Uyghur woman and a Han Chinese man (of the majority group in China) behind the counter. We identified her as Uyghur because of her wide face, sparkling bangles, and dangling earrings. (It was very rare for Han Chinese people to wear jewelry.) They were discussing a paper with a red seal on it. It appeared the Uyghur woman was unhappy about some kind of business deal. After they argued for a while, the man said in Chinese, "Drink a little tea and rest a while." The Uyghur woman, who had a cup of tea in her hand, tossed the tea on the floor, spat, and stomped out of the store.

ဖြၞ

Our destination was Lhasa, the center of Tibetan country, but we visited a thriving Tibetan Buddhist temple complex along the way. Taersi Lamasery was located about twenty-five miles from Xining, the capital of Qinghai province. The temple complex had a giant bronze pagoda, fierce-looking stuffed animals, prayer wheels, paper money stuck on trees, animal skins hung as offerings, elaborate yak-butter sculptures, burning candles, rugs wrapped around posts, and silk brocade strips hanging everywhere. Young Tibetans prostrated themselves before the main temple again and again. The images and smells boggled my mind because I had no reference point from which to interpret their meaning.

During our first evening at the temple complex, we encountered a middle-aged nomadic woman accompanied by a long-haired goat. She had short-cropped hair, was wrapped in thick orange and brown robes, and wore earrings of silver balls. The goat had brightly colored ribbons entwined in its neck hair. The woman was near the monastery, standing next to a tiny white tent and surrounded by a dozen disheveled children like a female Pied Piper. After we approached her, she held my hands in both of hers and chuckled deeply. She murmured in a tongue that was unfamiliar to me; she didn't seem to understand much Chinese.

As we interacted with Tibetans, we felt that they seemed to be less serious and more spontaneous than we had experienced many Han Chinese people to be, which delighted us. A Tibetan monk was fascinated by my portable umbrella. He took it from me and let me show him how to open it by pressing the button on the handle. Unable to figure out how to close it, he handed it back to me, still open.

At 5:30 the next morning, we were awakened by low-toned but loud horns. It so happened that we were visiting the monastery on the day of a religious festival. The celebration on this day was Turning the Sutra Wheel Three Times. At 8:30 a.m. the whole community of scarlet- and brown-robed monks—several hundred people—paraded past our guesthouse. Some blew horns, making music that sounded medieval to our ears. Most carried a rectangular wooden box tied shut with a silk band. The boxes contained sutra, or scripture. Sherri and I joined them, along with a number of Tibetan visitors, for a three-hour pilgrimage that wound up to the top of a mountain. At four different stops, the monks halted, opened their boxes, and chanted from the Tibetan script. They lit candles and turned prayer wheels, a string of large cylinders lined up on an outdoor frame.

Yellow Hat Tibetan Buddhist monks carry boxes of scripture in a processional at Taersi Monastery in Qinghai Province.

No one seemed to mind our being there. I asked one monk if it would be okay if we watched, and he said yes. Later when we were ready to move on to another station, he said, "Come on," in English. Another monk let me carry his scripture box. I explained I was a Christian, not a Buddhist, but he didn't seem to care. Even though we were the only white foreigners joining in the procession, everyone seemed unfazed by our presence.

A Tibetan woman was playful with us along the way. She teased me by stepping on the backs of my shoes from behind. She giggled when I turned around, and the women around her laughed at her harmless trick. Sherri and I chatted with a Tibetan man from New York City who was visiting the monastery for the festival and spoke English. He introduced us to his two sisters. The women, who were from Golmud, wore traditional Tibetan clothing—long dresses. Their hair was braided in dozens of tiny, long braids, and the women smelled of yak butter.

৩৶৶

After Sherri and I embarked on the part of the trip beyond where the train line stopped in Golmud, we traveled over terrible muddy roads with some sections that had been washed out. Our bus was navigated by a Tibetan man who definitely seemed to have a high-risk gene. The bus often tipped to one side or the other so dramatically that we feared it would turn over. Sometimes it got stuck, and we all pitched in to toss rocks around the tires for traction.

The scenery was spectacular during our journey over the high plateau. We caught a gorgeous view of the Tanggula Mountains, the foothills of the Himalayan Mountains. I later wrote a haiku about the scenery:

> Blue snowy peaks rise
> above pink cloud seas greeting
> a Tibetan dawn.

On the bus, two Tibetan women befriended us. I learned how to say "hello" and "good-bye" in their language. Unlike the Chinese people we knew, who seemed to feel obliged to offer us delicacies, the Tibetan women offered simple food such as noodles, tea, and watermelon. The women advocated for Sherri and me at our dank adobe hotel by reclaiming our beds for us; some truckers had taken them over when we had gone out for dinner to the home of a Hui Chinese family, the closest thing to a restaurant.

The women also later found us in Lhasa and took us spontaneously to their home. Sherri and I were not accustomed to this kind of informality in China, and it was very welcome.

Buddhist pilgrims prostrate themselves in front of the Jokhang Temple
in Lhasa in 1987.

We explored Lhasa on foot, amazed by all the evidence around us of the devotion of Tibetans to religious practice. I hadn't witnessed that kind of collective religious fervor in my China experience. When Tibetans I met saw the photo of the Dalai Lama, the religious leader of the Tibetans, in my Lonely Planet China guidebook, they touched the photo to their foreheads in respect. At the main Buddhist temple in the center of Lhasa, called the Jokhang, Tibetan pilgrims from different regions—including men wearing colorful red-fringed headwear—circled the temple on foot. Once, when we were circling the temple, a girl took my hand and playfully tried to mimic my speech. When Sherri and I took a day trip outside of Lhasa to visit the Tibetan Buddhist monastery of Drepung, the monks welcomed us to join the thousand or so worshippers by sitting cross-legged on a mat. They insisted on our drinking yak-butter tea with *tsampa* (barley flour) during the service. Here I had a reference point. I likened the action to taking communion in the Christian tradition.

I wonder whether the attraction to Tibetan Buddhism for many Westerners lies in part in the seemingly inclusive and also playful, informal culture of Tibetans. It did provide a sharp contrast to the culture of the majority group in China—the Han Chinese people. I later wrote a poem reflecting on my visit to the Jokhang temple:

Spiritual Circuit

I find myself at dusk
walking round and round
the Jokhang temple.
Tibetans make room
for Western misfits
on the spiritual path
between whitewashed buildings.

Round and round
carried on by the rhythmic
hum of prayers
encouraged by the smiles
of turquoise-laden women.
The only rule is to
walk clockwise
and there is no destination.

31

Chinese Students in the United States
Respond to Tiananmen

Mary Ann

As I TRANSITIONED BACK to life in my home country, I recognized that the knowledge that my Luzhou students and teaching colleagues had shared with me about China was a *huge* gift. Because China is such an important country in the world and not many Americans had been there in the 1980s, people were curious about what I'd experienced and learned. The gift was invaluable as I started a new phase in my life as a student in the graduate journalism program at Indiana University in Bloomington for the 1988–1989 academic year.

It wasn't hard to find opportunities to apply my knowledge about China. I reported for the local Bloomington newspaper on a visit to campus by the prominent Chinese writer and intellectual Liu Binyan. In the 1950s, Liu had been put out of the Communist Party because of a report he wrote that criticized the construction of a bridge over the Yellow River.[1] Then in 1978, he had been reinstated to the party, only to be expelled again in 1987, at the same time that Hu Yaobang was ousted, right before Fran and I embarked on our travels in China during the Spring Festival. In his speech on campus, Liu called on the Chinese Communist Party to support an independent newspaper in which writers could freely express their views.

1. Zehr, "Chinese Writer," 4.

Suddenly, the opportunities to localize stories about a changing China exploded. Chinese undergraduate students started marching in Beijing and demanding "democracy." From April and onward through 1989, I kept up with my journalism courses, but my intellect and interactions with other people were focused on reporting on how Chinese graduate students in the United States responded to students occupying Tiananmen Square. Indiana University had 137 students from mainland China that school year; about forty thousand Chinese students were enrolled in universities across the United States.[2] A decade before, almost zero Chinese people were studying in U.S. universities.

On the other side of the globe from Indiana, Beijing students erected a reproduction of the Statue of Liberty in Tiananmen Square to symbolize that they were calling for Western-style democracy. Students held hunger strikes. At the peak of the protests hundreds of thousands of people, including workers, flooded the streets of Beijing demanding reforms by the Chinese Communist Party.

Because of my China experience, the Chinese students on the Bloomington campus seemed to trust me. They invited me to tag along with a carload of students on a Saturday in May 1989; these students joined about three thousand mainland Chinese students to show support for the students in Tiananmen Square with demonstrations in front of the Chinese consulate in Chicago. They rallied outside the consulate shouting, "Li Peng must go!"[3] The students perceived Li Peng, the prime minister of China at the time, to be opposed to democracy. I reported on the students' protests for *The Indianapolis Star*.

Tanks rolled in on Tiananmen Square, clearing the square of protestors and killing hundreds of civilians on June 3 and 4. An American journalist who was an eyewitness estimated that between four hundred and eight hundred civilians were killed, as well as about a dozen soldiers and police.[4] (The Chinese Communist Party eventually rewarded the soldiers who died while clearing the square by declaring them party members posthumously.)[5]

The Chinese students at Indiana University responded with anger and grief. They organized a memorial service in Bloomington on June 11 for

2. Zehr, "Chinese Students at IU," A-1.

3. Zehr, "Students at Colleges," para. 2.

4. Kristof, "A Reassessment," para. 3.

5. Rosen, "The Impact of Reform Policies," 295.

the Beijing students who had been killed. More than five hundred people attended, including a state politician.

"What could they do but bathe the square in their own blood and litter the streets with their bodies?" cried out Zhu Jian-Hua, an Indiana University graduate student from Shanghai and a speaker at the service.[6]

"The government [in China] says this is the beginning of suppression," said Lu Xiaopeng, another Indiana University graduate student at the service. "We say this is the beginning of our fight for democracy."[7]

Several weeks after the memorial service, He Zhou, a 35-year-old doctoral student in journalism, tipped me off that he and several other students planned to join more than two hundred Chinese students studying in the United States in resigning from the Communist Party to denounce how the Chinese leaders had killed students.

He Zhou told me that the Communist Party had advised students not to admit their membership in the party when they applied for visas to study in the United States. But to protest the Tiananmen Square killings, he said, students "identify themselves as Communists only for the purpose of quitting."[8] He Zhou resigned from the party after five years of membership.

Before graduate school, He Zhou was a journalist for Xinhua, China's most important news agency and a mouthpiece for the Chinese government. Party membership gave him access to high-level meetings of government leaders, he explained to me. His resignation meant giving up a successful career; it was a big risk.

"We cannot do many things to protest [the massacre]," Pan Youfang, 39, a graduate student in computer science at Indiana University, said. "This is one thing we can do." He added, "The Communist Party no longer represents the people." Pan Youfang resigned from the party after sixteen years of membership.

In the fall, Chinese students on U.S. campuses, including Indiana University, were still organizing; from Beijing, Chinese leaders were trying to shut down those efforts. The *People's Daily*, a media tool of the Chinese government, published admonitions to Chinese people living in the United States: those who protested at a planned rally in Washington, DC, in October would be considered "enemies of the people."[9] The warnings caused

6. Zehr, "Chinese Students Grieve," A-1.

7. Zehr, "Chinese Students Grieve," A-6.

8. Zehr, "Chinese Students in U.S. Renounce," C-4.

9. Zehr, "D.C. Rally to Defy," A-1.

the number of Chinese students at Indiana University who had signed up to travel to the rally to drop—from fifty to thirty, I reported in the *Indianapolis Star*, which by then had hired me as a reporting intern. In a phone interview, a student from Kent State University in Ohio told me that an official from the Chinese consulate in New York City had telephoned him and tried to persuade him not to join the rally in DC.

I called the Chinese consulate in New York City to get a comment from someone representing the Chinese government. The secretary to the consul general of the New York consulate, Wu Xiao Zhong, told me over the phone that if any Chinese officials had called students, "it would just be friendly talk, not intimidation."[10] He said he wasn't aware of any articles in the *People's Daily* referring to the Washington rally. He added: "To be frank, I haven't had time to read the papers these days." I put those exact words in the news article about the planned rally.

There was no stopping He Zhou. He said his anger toward editorials in the *People's Daily* spurred him to sign up for the rally, two weeks before the qualifying examinations for his doctoral degree. "I have said to hell with my qualifying exams. I have to go to show my defiance to the reactionary regime," he said.[11]

The students who had joined the party and then defied the party had my respect. I'd seen enough of China to understand the risks they were taking.

৬৫৬

In Luzhou, something happened that could have been a ripple effect from a change in the political climate created across China by the crisis in Tiananmen Square. The Luzhou Medical College leaders reversed their policy of encouraging students to take the TOEFL test, a standardized English test that could enable them to go abroad to study medicine and technology. In a letter dated December 8, 1989, Zhang Dongni shared disheartening news:

> Our college has made statement that TOEFL exam is canceled. Nobody can take TOEFL exam. Though I work in this college and Lin, director of FAO [foreign affairs office], has been to abroad once, I have to recognize our college leaders are very conservative.

10. Zehr, "D.C. Rally to Defy Alarms from China," A-5.
11. Zehr, "D.C. Rally to Defy Alarms from China," A-5.

Unlike Chengdu, Chongqing, big cities, their leaders encourage the students to take part in TOEFL exam. Our leaders are afraid that once we go abroad, we don't come back to college even though we pledge. We just test our English level, not go abroad. This is China!

32

Ling Ling: A Dream Meets Reality

Mary Ann

SOMETHING WE DIDN'T ANTICIPATE was that two of our former students would migrate to the United States. We have become lifelong friends. Zhang Dongni, our former student who became our interpreter and closest friend in Luzhou, moved to Guam and then to California. Ling Ling is another former student who moved to the United States. She is a nurse who studied in our intensive English course in Luzhou for two semesters.

When she was our student, Ling Ling was only 20 years old. She had bright eyes and an engaging smile. Ling Ling was confident in practicing her spoken English, but during our days in Luzhou, our conversations were superficial. She was a friend of Zhang Dongni and sometimes accompanied Zhang to our apartment. Ling Ling migrated to a large northeastern American city in 1997, and she and I have exchanged visits seven times. She became a U.S. citizen in 2010.

ক৸৶

About a half year after I left Luzhou, Ling Ling sent me a letter describing her passion for English study and expressing a desire to come to the United States. When she wrote the letter in January 1988, she was awaiting the results of a standardized English test. She eventually learned she had passed it.

Fran and I really underestimated how many of our students would be able to pass standardized English tests and study abroad. In the years after we left Luzhou, we heard about former students who were studying in Denmark, Canada, Australia, and Japan. Ling Ling wrote: "No one [from Luzhou] has gone to U.S.A. until now to join you. I'll make an effort to meet you in America (laughing)."

Although she indicated with the parenthetical comment that she might be joking, she was actually very serious about her goal of leaving China. Ling Ling said that she hoped I was not too busy to sit down and write a letter to her, saying, "You are the one American lady I've known."

I wrote Ling Ling back, and I sent her a world almanac, which I thought could be useful for English study. In a June 1988 letter, Ling Ling again mentioned her desire to go abroad. She wrote: "I haven't any chance to go abroad at least now. Because I was less educated and not well-experienced. I have to make extra effort to reach the permitting level to [go] abroad."

After I moved a few times, I lost contact with Ling Ling, but we resumed writing letters in 1995 after Zhang Dongni tracked down my Washington, DC, address and shared it with Ling Ling. Fran and I were both living in DC then. Interestingly, at this point Ling Ling had migrated to the United Arab Emirates and was in her third year working as a nurse in a hospital there. She'd carried out her plan to go abroad. But emotional adjustment hadn't been easy. She wrote that she felt "extremely alone" away from her friends and family.

A couple of years later, Ling Ling said in a letter that she had spent five "long, boring and lonely years" in the United Arab Emirates. She wrote: "I always want to come to States. But the visa is not easy to acquire. I wonder why American government will refuse us Chinese. I wish I could find a job there, so I can enjoy the beauty of the American life."

In an unexpected turn of events, in August 1997, Ling Ling accomplished her dream. She got a work visa for a job to be a private nurse for a patient receiving care in the United States.

Ling Ling and I were eager to see each other face-to-face. My then husband and I traveled by plane to spend a weekend with her in her new city. She soon also visited us in Washington, DC, and we took in the White House and other sights together.

It was in those first years in the United States that Ling Ling's loneliness led to her becoming a Christian. She was out on a walk and came across a building with some Chinese characters. She didn't initially know it was a church, but she ended up connecting with people of Chinese heritage there. In 1999, Ling Ling was baptized as a Christian.

After her initial job in the United States ended, Ling Ling landed another one, working in a nursing home with Cantonese-speaking patients. She had passed the exam to be a registered nurse in the United States, and she continued to study and improve her technical skills. She is now a nurse for cancer patients in a prestigious institution. Her work is fulfilling. "I love my patients," she says.

Whenever we met up in the United States, Ling Ling was very open in our conversations. She was thoughtful and straightforward in her opinions. I enjoyed her good sense of humor, which she employed when telling stories about navigating a new country.

I was sad to learn that Ling Ling experienced discrimination in the workplace. Some patients complained about her accent. Coworkers sometimes discriminated against her. I felt angry when I heard these stories. She actually speaks English fluently, and her accent doesn't impede communication. But I was also inspired by how she advocated for herself in trying situations.

It has been challenging for Ling Ling to make friends with Americans. Her American coworkers at the hospital have been very busy, and they haven't socialized much with her outside of work. Particularly in her first few years in the United States, she felt socially isolated in a way that was similar to what Fran and I felt in Luzhou. During her visit to my home in 2008, a decade after she had settled in the United States, Ling Ling told my then husband and me, "You are my only American friends."

Ling Ling's statement made me feel sad and spoke to me of what seemed to be the unwillingness of some Americans to get to know people who were from a culture different from their own and to welcome them into their circles.

33

Heart and Home: The Door Is Open

FRAN

WHEN I LEFT CHINA in February 1988, I knew that Zhang Dongni had been dating a well-connected young man, a relationship she was prodded into because she had become rather fiercely independent (with our influence perhaps partly to blame). She got married and had a daughter. Later Zhang wrote that she was divorced and had left her daughter in the care of the child's grandparents.

After Zhang moved to Kunming in 1993, she wrote that she loved the relative freedom there, out from under the smothering climate of Luzhou. She elaborated on the way she felt in a letter to us:

> In Kunming, I really feel free, no pressure in my heart, not like in
> Luzhou, always worry about my talking and action with foreigners
> and working. When I remember it, I feel sad. Also, Luzhou's peo-
> ple still feel restraint about FAO [foreign affairs office]. As a result
> of this, no native-speaking English would like to go to Luzhou at
> present. The college invites French and Japanese to teach English.

After the spring semester of 1989, CEE had stopped sending any teachers to Luzhou. The organization saw a sharp drop in the number of teachers wanting to go to China after the widely publicized crackdown on protestors in Tiananmen Square. In addition, the CEE teachers who were assigned to teach in Luzhou after we left had apparently clashed with Teacher Lin and the *waiban* even more than we had. (After the foreign affairs office had new leadership—nearly ten years later, in 1998—CEE once again resumed assigning teachers to Luzhou Medical College.) We have learned that Teacher Lin died in 2006 from cancer.

\ෙ෭෪

In Kunming, Zhang got to know more Westerners and converted to Christianity. Zhang regularly attended English Corner, meetings organized by Chinese Americans for Chinese young people to meet and interact with Americans and other foreigners in order to improve their English. Sometimes participants would watch and discuss movies together. Zhang listed the ones she liked: *Mrs. Doubtfire*, *Sleepless in Seattle*, *A Woman's Scent*, and others. She wrote that every day, about one hundred Americans came to Kunming, many of them students and teachers. Zhang wrote, perhaps tongue-in-cheek, "We discuss and talk about many interesting things but because, some reason, we avoid talking about the government and political problems." As she continued to interact with Americans, she wrote, "I know your country more and more, better and better. It's really a great difference."

It was at an English Corner event that Zhang met an American woman whose father was apparently a famous pastor in the United States. Her new friend provided pamphlets and information about the Bible. She also gave lectures about the Bible in English. Zhang wrote of this newfound love:

> I study Bible in Chinese and in English every three days, sometimes with Americans, sometimes with Chinese friends. I go to church every Sunday morning. Since I became a Christianity last year, I feel peace in my mind. I believe in God, Christ and reading, studying, discussing in group Bible (study) with my friends. But when we gather together, we are careful and secretly. We don't want to cause too much trouble. Although the government permits free-religion, it is not permitted gathering and spreading Bible.

Zhang wrote to us about her impression of Christians that she met: "I feel they are very kindness and filled-love to people. I also often like according to the aspects of Christianity growing, molding a good personality . . . I feel rich colorful life, not empty in my heart at all."

More than a decade after I returned to the United States, I found out to my surprise that Zhang was living fairly close to me, working in a Chinese restaurant in a coastal California town! My husband, Ken, and I went to visit her in the summer of 2005. She gave us tasteful T-shirts from her restaurant, black with red chopsticks on them, and we spent the day at a beachside park, reliving old times and learning about her new life in the United States.

Several years later, our family visited Zhang again. This time she was the full owner of a Chinese restaurant in another lovely little tourist town in northern California. I was so excited and proud of how Zhang had built a life for herself and was now a valued member of the local community.

34

2019: Raising a Glass to Friendship in the City of Wine

FRAN

WHEN I REVISITED LUZHOU on that warm summer day in 2019, I found myself back on the medical school campus, trudging up the familiar steps more than thirty years after I had last mounted them. As we were climbing, our local guide suddenly turned to me and asked a simple question that should not have thrown me but did: "Is there anyone you would want to see while you are here?"

For some reason, I had had the idea that after more than three decades, not one person would be left in Luzhou whom I would know or who would be interested in seeing me. But two names leaped immediately to mind: those of our former student, Hu Bing, and the stylish English teacher, Teacher Lu. To my surprise, Teacher Wang knew them and how to get in touch with them. She said she would try to arrange a time to meet up, maybe even for lunch.

My mind was filled with a flurry of memories as we continued up the steps—the ones we used to trudge up after we had bought vegetables and fruit from the marketplace below. As we turned onto the campus proper, I looked around keenly. Mary Ann and I had walked every pathway there was around the campus, buying chocolate and cheap wine, reminiscing about home, and analyzing our students' personalities and the comments they made to us. The stone lions guarding the gate reminded me of the pictures Mary Ann and I had taken there to send back home on a day when we were bored and trying to think of something to do to fill the time. And there was the movie theater, where a young teacher had sat between us and translated a kung fu film, only to be scolded later.

At last, we reached our former apartment block. On this day the complex was partitioned off from its courtyard with a heavy wire fence. The place where we had lived seemed smaller than I remembered it. No one seemed to be living there.

In fact, as I looked around, almost no one seemed to be living anywhere. The campus was vacant, left to fall into disrepair, with moldy walls and walkways, fading into the dull green of the camphor trees surrounding it. A few student shirts and pants hanging from some apartment balconies were the only signs of life there. I had reentered a past that was no longer there. As I learned later, nearly all teachers, students, and staff had been relocated to the spanking new medical college down the hill, near the Yangtze River. Only a few traditional medicine students remained.

After taking a few quick pictures, we were ready to descend the hill, get in our guide's car, and drive to the new campus, now called Southwest Medical University. It welcomed us with wide gates and avenues, green lawn (grass! Something we never saw during our time in Luzhou), fountains, bridges, and a trendy-looking pagoda from which we could survey the smart-looking office buildings, teacher complex, and state-of-the art sports fields. Everything felt expansive, sparkling, and full of possibility.

We wandered around a bit, covering only a small fraction of the campus, unlike how we had just walked the whole mountain campus in minutes, and our guide picked us up to take us to lunch. And here was the real homecoming. As we walked up the restaurant stairs and down a corridor to our banquet room, I nearly passed by a figure standing to the side. Then, glimpsing her face, I stopped. It was the English teacher, Teacher Lu, classy as always in a flowing green dress—though without her youthful glow—long strings of black hair framing her face. She greeted us with a quizzical smile. We were all shy, so it was handshakes, not hugs, and then she made a gesture for us to enter a room set up for our group.

Already seated in the corner—my heart leaped—was my dearly beloved former student, Hu Bing. His round, beaming face looked the same, not much older. Here he was, one of our most earnest students, who had been eager to open his life to the outside world. Did he ever get the chance?

At the table were our local guide, Hu Bing, Teacher Lu, and one other person I did not recognize—a formal representative of the school administration, no doubt, sent out to watch over us.

As we ate spicy Sichuan chicken and *jiaozi*, Hu Bing sat at my left elbow, keeping up a steady conversation the whole time. "Did you know I was abroad for four years? I was in charge of a medical project there. It was wonderful. I hope to go abroad to retire, but I don't know if I can get the chance." I asked about his family and he got out a picture. After another bite or two of food, he continued, "You know I tried to get into an American university? I tried three times, but I failed. It was a dream, but I cannot go." As the conversation picked up, I was surprised to realize that Hu Bing was still quite fluent in English after all these years. He said, "My friend is the director of our department now. He and I were college classmates. He became the director and moved over to the new campus ten years ago. I moved over last year. The new teacher apartments are very nice." There was something that I could not read in his eyes but could feel, even though he smiled as he spoke. "But now I really want to say thank you—thank you for teaching me English and giving me so much opportunity to improve my life." His eyes were bright as he looked at me.

I felt at that moment that I had been handed all the reward I ever needed. "I was honored to have such good students!" I responded sincerely.

Then I looked across the table at Teacher Lu sitting so calmly, remembering the fiery young woman we had encountered as part of the English Department faculty so many years ago. I knew that she had married while we were still in Luzhou. As was the case with most of the young people who selected a life partner while we were there, we hadn't known she was dating anyone. I also knew that she later was one of those lucky people who had given birth to twins, the only way to get around the government's one-child-only policy. Now, when I asked her about her life, she spoke in beautiful English.

"Oh, I am the head of the foreign affairs office. I meet regularly with the foreign teachers. Yes, we have several. I am lucky. I have traveled all over the world for my job. I have even been to California—Los Angeles. I have two sons. When I retire, I want to go live with them in Chengdu. That is the city where your group is now, yes? My sons both have nice lives in Chengdu." She sighed, "Such a modern city."

I looked at her, incredulous. Not so much because she was planning to move to the big city soon, but because she had been able to travel out of

China at all! Here she was, director of the foreign affairs office, a coveted position, and a world traveler as well. I never expected her life to be so expansive, so apparently satisfying. She seemed so serene sitting there, even queenly. Both she and Hu Bing, though still working in the traditional, conservative city of Luzhou, had clearly risen in the ranks and had been afforded opportunities I never would have imagined.

As we walked out of the restaurant, Teacher Lu pressed a package into my hands. "I hope you like it," she murmured. It was a beautiful jade incense bowl with wrought-iron sides and several pieces of incense carefully wrapped in colored paper. I breathed my thanks, and before I knew it, we were exchanging contact numbers and waving goodbye.

"Don't wait thirty years to come back!" Hu Bing was saying as our guide's car drove up. "Come back soon. Come back next year and bring Mary Ann with you."

"I will try, I really will," I said, and meant it, though a part of me felt like I had had my homecoming, had come around full circle, had finally closed the loop. I had seen progress, newness, and a measure of hope. Knowing China, knowing the ever-changing political climate, knowing that there is often something hard and suffocating, unspoken but just under the surface, I was not sure how hopeful to be, but I willed with all my heart for China and its people to have a bright future.

35

Virtual Reunions
with Our Chinese Friends

FRAN AND MARY ANN

IN A MARCH 2021 Zoom call, we renewed our friendship with Ling Ling and shared memories about our time in Luzhou. Ling Ling recalled that she had wondered whether we had been lonely. She thought we must have missed our families and other Americans. She said, "I wonder how you survived." She added, "We wanted to have more friendship. You were friendly, easy-going, approachable."

Ling Ling told us that she is still a Christian: "I know God is leading me up to now," she said. We asked if she had known that Luzhou had a church. She said that after we left Luzhou, she had visited the church once with a friend who attended. Her purpose was to interact in English with the foreign people in attendance. We mentioned to Ling Ling that a Christian organization had sent us to Luzhou. We shared that Mary Ann had had unresolved doubts about Christianity while living in Luzhou. Ling Ling said she thought our faith had come through in our teaching.

Ling Ling still has a strong connection to China. Her mother and brother live in Chengdu; in retirement, she anticipates living in both the United States and China.

She said, "People ask, 'Why did you leave your country?'" She told us that she responds, "In the 1980s, China was so underdeveloped. I lived with five people in a room. I didn't have a shower or kitchen. I had to go to the public bath and dining hall."

She added that now some of her nursing colleagues from long ago in Luzhou have a standard of living in China that is higher than her own in the United States. Whereas Ling Ling currently has no car and lives in a tiny condominium, some of her Chinese colleagues live in two- or three-bedroom apartments. One of her classmates in Luzhou drives a Mercedes.

♾

A few months after the virtual reunion with Ling Ling, we arranged a FaceTime chat with Zhang Dongni. When we all appeared on the screen, Zhang was suddenly animated. "Mary! Frans! I see you!" We laughed and settled down for a long chat. Even though it was late and Zhang had bills and accounting to do (she calls herself a workaholic), she dismissed that work with a wave. "I can do later. Let's talk."

What followed was a conversation about our Luzhou experience and about her experience as well, punctuated with surprise, frowns, laughter, and a general feeling of overwhelming love for each other. The main take-away from our talk was that Zhang had indeed been caught in the middle between the foreigners and the foreign affairs office—and that she had decided to trust us and side with us when push came to shove. "I talk to you both. I love you very much," Zhang said. "I'm always on your side." The bravery and strong moral fiber of her character shone through in a way that amazed us, even knowing her as we did. We were the first foreigners she had ever met. When we asked why she trusted us, she said that she felt we were "so honest—so pure at that time. No fake."

We discussed how difficult it was for Zhang to work for the foreign affairs office—how she often refused when she was asked to lie about what we said or did. How she had to uphold the restrictions on student-teacher relationships because the officials were afraid the students would tell us too much or that we might have a romantic relationship with someone. These restrictions extended to her behavior. When she invited us to her house for dinner one night, Teacher Lin was displeased, forbidding her to talk to us about anything important. "He found we had a good relationship. I told you everything," Zhang said. We were awed and humbled. Zhang had invited us over even when told not to. She had stood up to her boss and taken the consequences. At the same time, she had handed us one of our favorite memories of being in Luzhou—an intimate family dinner at the house of our friend.

161

In our call, we were delighted to hear that Zhang was a U.S. citizen and had, in fact, become one ten years previously.

Zhang has never returned to Luzhou since she has been living in the United States, even though she has visited China several times. "I didn't go to Luzhou for over twenty years," she said. "I went to Kunming."

As we hung up the phone, our hearts were full. We admired Zhang even more now that we knew the extent of all the battles she had had to fight for us, and we felt a renewed sense of warmth toward her. Talking with Zhang had put us back in that shadowed world of secrets, claustrophobic restrictions, and speculation, but it had also opened us up to the true beauty of someone we had grown to love and admire and with whom we planned to continue to connect for a lifetime.

It is not much of a stretch to say that we survived in Luzhou because of Zhang Dongni. She was the one we leaned on, heavily, during our time there. She enlivened our world and made it palatable. And so did other students like Ling Ling, Hu Bing, and Yan Jian as well as Luzhou faculty like Teacher Lu, Teacher Bai, and Teachers Fu and Tang. We came to know and love our Chinese friends in our sojourn in Luzhou. Despite some miscommunications and frustrations, the friendships and relationships we built together are the true keepsakes we brought home from China.

In the 1980s, the door in China was cracked open so that we, as ordinary Americans, had the opportunity to interact with ordinary Chinese people. Since then, that door has swung open wider and then seemingly begun to close again. Our experiences show that educational exchange is a way of opening up possibilities. This way is not dramatic, but it is effective.

It seemed that the *waiban* officials wanted us to be a simple mechanism for transferring skills and language to better the future of Luzhou Medical College students. However, with human interaction, that kind of automation is never possible. Thoughts, feelings, dreams, yearnings, philosophy, spirituality, and much more come into play and cannot be squelched. Personal exchanges bring together person to person, mind to mind, and heart to heart. Nothing can take the place of that kind of human connection.

Afterword

FRAN AND MARY ANN

OUR FRIENDSHIP WAS SPARKED in Goshen, took shape in Honduras, was tried by fire in China, and continued afterward in DC and elsewhere. It was deepened and fortified by our shared joys and challenges of living in Luzhou. Our different personalities complemented each other. Mary Ann forged ahead to clarify and confront problems. She pushed the envelope, asking probing and insightful questions to our students and fellow teachers. Fran provided calm and a tempering tone when discussions with college leaders got heated. Her tendency to be patient and take time to read a situation and then come up with a thoughtful diplomatic response was also often needed because it helped us to build trust with the Chinese people.

Mary Ann and Fran in the stone forest in Sichuan Province in 1986

It was true that the intensity of our living situation in a Chinese closed city tested our friendship. One time that our friendship showed some strain was at the end of our first semester in Luzhou. We had left Luzhou that semester only once to visit the larger city of Chengdu. We were weary of having to do everything together, and some small annoyances had worked their way into our relationship. But then came the summer break, which gave us breathing room as we studied the Chinese language in Nanjing with other American and Canadian teachers. Afterward, Fran traveled south to Kunming with some of the teachers and Mary Ann took a train north to see her former Chinese teacher in Beijing. By the time the fall semester started, our appreciation for and solidarity with each other had been renewed.

After we returned to the United States, the 1990s was a rich time for our friendship. For seven years, we lived a few miles from each other in the DC area. Fran and her husband, Ken, attended graduate school and started a family; Mary Ann worked as an editor and then a journalist. It was common for us to go to the theater together or meet up in coffee shops or in each other's homes for meals or parties. Fran and Ken and their firstborn, then a toddler, attended Mary Ann's wedding, and Fran stood up with the wedding couple as an official witness. Mary Ann kept Fran company in the hospital just before she gave birth to her second child when her family members took breaks to get meals.

And then in 2017, Fran convinced Mary Ann to join her and Ken in Bangkok, Thailand, where they took a group of university students for a learning tour. In Bangkok, we spent a lovely evening as a twosome, celebrating Mary Ann's birthday. We got soaked in monsoon rains, reminisced over dinner in a restaurant, and toasted each other while sipping pricey drinks at a "sky bar," looking down on Bangkok's skyscrapers as dusk turned the city into twinkling lights. Mary Ann then also traveled in Vietnam with Ken and Fran, who had organized a tour for their friends, drawing on the knowledge of Vietnam they had acquired while living and working there for five years.

ฝฟผ

To this very day, we know aspects of each other's personalities in a way that siblings often do. Mary Ann is stubborn but will reverse her position if faced with a strong argument and then she regrets that she dug in her heels. Fran knows how to make those arguments! And Fran also knows how to lighten things up so we have fun. Our shared traits of intellectual curiosity, an adventuresome spirit, an ability to be present in the moment, and a desire to express warmth toward each other and people we meet make up the foundation of our friendship.

Mary Ann initiated the project of co-writing a memoir in January 2021, after finding a stash of letters that she had written from Luzhou to her parents. The lockdown of the pandemic gave us time to write, and for more than a year we churned out chapters and frequently jumped on the phone to process memories and give feedback. Mary Ann's research about China and her ideas for how to organize the book benefited the project as did Fran's talent for descriptive writing and communicating emotion. We sometimes argued about the writing, and some of the old patterns in our friendship resurfaced. Mary Ann would get fixed on a certain approach, and then Fran would find a way to convince her she should open up her thinking. (For example, Fran insisted that the memoir include photographs.). In turn, Mary Ann kept Fran true to actual dates, places, and events, honing in on her journalistic instincts.

Fran made the project fun by inviting Mary Ann to travel from her home in Virginia to Fran's stomping ground in California for a "writers' retreat" in a cottage near Yosemite National Park in the summer of 2022. We worked on the memoir for a day at the cottage and spent another day hiking up to a waterfall in the park. The memoir has given us a reason to meet in person several other times as well.

It has been a healing process to revisit the memories of Luzhou. A dark cloudiness had lingered for decades in our subconscious about our experiences there. Mary Ann questioned whether her experiences in Luzhou could have been more rewarding if she had more effectively studied the Chinese language or tried even harder to get around the rules that hindered meaningful interactions with Chinese people. Fran had a measure of frustration and even resentment toward the Chinese officials who she felt had needlessly squelched opportunities for connections between people. She noted that when she lived and worked in Vietnam from 1997 to 2002, she didn't experience the same kind of restrictions that she had in China, despite the fact that Vietnam was also a Communist country.

In our conversations with each other and in reconnecting with Zhang Dongni and Ling Ling, we started to understand better the context of the 1980s in China. We offered a kind of grace to our younger selves and to Chinese officials who we had perceived as having been overzealous in managing our lives. We came to a point in which we honored the creativity and persistence we had practiced in Luzhou and recognized that some of our Chinese students and teaching colleagues had also been remarkably innovative and persistent in pursuing friendships with us. We are grateful we supported each other then, and we celebrate how we have sustained our friendship for four rich and rewarding decades.

Fran and Mary Ann in 2021 (photo by Randi B. Hagi)

A Glossary
of Chinese Words and Phrases

Food and Drink

baijiu (rice wine)

chaoshou (a kind of dumpling)

jiaozi (pork dumpling)

mala (spicy)

mapo doufu (combination of pork, tofu, peanuts, and spicy sauce)

Other Items and Expressions

bu hao kan (not beautiful)

da bizi (people with big noses)

Cesuo zai nar (Where is the bathroom?)

didi (little brother)

jin (pound)

man zou (walk slowly, a farewell to guests)

meiyou (not have, a common response to questions about items for purchase)

neige (um, you know, a filler word in conversation)

Ni chi fan le ma (Have you eaten yet? A common greeting in the morning, taken from the hard times in China's history when food was sometimes scarce). Answers: *Chi le* (I've eaten) or *Meiyou chi* (I haven't eaten)

meimei (little sister)

Ni hao (Hello)

Nide shenti hen hao (your health is good, dubbing our exercise teacher)

putonghua (Mandarin; common language)

renminbi (local Chinese currency vs. FEC, the currency foreigners used)

taiji (a form of martial art used as daily exercise routine)

waiban (foreign affairs office)

waiguoren (foreigner; people from the outside)

Wode mingzi shi . . . (My name is . . .)

Wu Zetian (popular TV historical drama about an empress in the Tang Dynasty)

yangguizi (foreign devil or ghost; offensive word for foreigner)

yuan (Chinese currency unit; Chinese dollar)

Bibliography

Burkholder, J. Lawrence. *Recollections of a Sectarian Realist: A Mennonite Life in the Twentieth Century.* Edited by Myrna Burkholder. Elkhart, IN: Institute of Mennonite Studies, Anabaptist Mennonite Biblical Seminary, 2016.

———. "Rethinking Christian Life and Mission in Light of the Chinese Experience." In *China and Christianity: Historical and Future Encounters*, edited by James D. Whitehead, Yuming Shaw, and N. J. Girardot, 206–28. Notre Dame: The Center for Pastoral and Social Ministry, the University of Notre Dame, 1979.

Consulate General of the United States of America. "Important Notice for American Citizens." In the authors' possession, September 16, 1987.

Davis, Deborah, and Ezra F. Vogel. "Introduction: The Social and Political Consequences of Reforms." In *Chinese Society on the Eve of Tiananmen: The Impact of Reform*, edited by Deborah Davis and Ezra F. Vogel, 1–12. Boston: Harvard University Asia Center, 1990.

Gargan, Edward A. "Thousands Stage Rally in Shanghai Demanding Rights." *New York Times*, December 21, 1986.

———. "Warning by China's Police Cool Protests by Students." *New York Times*, December 23, 1986.

Hessler, Peter. *River Town: Two Years on the Yangtze.* New York: HarperCollins, 2001.

———. "The Peace Corps Breaks Ties with China." *New Yorker*, March 9, 2020. https://www.newyorker.com/magazine/2020/03/16/the-peace-corps-breaks-ties-with-china.

Kristof, Nicholas D. "A Reassessment of How Many Died in the Military Crackdown in Beijing." *New York Times*, June 21, 1989.

Madsen, Richard. "The Spiritual Crisis of China's Intellectuals." In *Chinese Society on the Eve of Tiananmen: The Impact of Reform*, edited by Deborah Davis and Ezra F. Vogel, 243–60. Boston: Harvard University Asia Center, 1990.

Missionary Society of the Methodist Church. *Our West China Mission: Being a Somewhat Extensive Summary by the Missionaries of the Field of the Work during the First Twenty-Five Years of the Canadian Methodist Mission in the Province of Szechwan, Western China.* Toronto: The Missionary Society of the Methodist Church, Young People's Forward Movement, 1920.

Reilly, Thomas H. *The Taiping Heavenly Kingdom: Rebellion and the Blasphemy of Empire.* Seattle: University of Washington Press, 2004.

Rosen, Stanley. "The Impact of Reform Policies on Youth Attitudes." In *Chinese Society on the Eve of Tiananmen: The Impact of Reform*, edited by Deborah Davis and Ezra F. Vogel, 283–305. Boston: Harvard University Asia Center, 1990.

Samagalski, Alan, and Michael Buckley. *China: A Travel Survival Kit*. South Yarra, Victoria, Australia: Lonely Planet, 1984.

Song, Zhuoying. "A Study of Three Women Missionaries of the United Church of Canada, from the Maritime Provinces to Sichuan, China, 1933–1952." Master's thesis, Saint Mary's University, May 1993. ProQuest.

"Summary of a Conversation with Fran Martens and Mary Ann Zehr, Luzhou, Sichuan Province, March 9, 1987." Prepared by A. C. Lobe. Mennonite Partners in Education archives, n.d.

"Summary of Visit to the Luzhou Medical College Luzhou City, Sichuan Province, October 23 & 24, 1985." Mennonite Partners in Education archives, n.d.

Wickeri, Philip L. *Reconstructing Christianity in China: K. H. Ting and the Chinese Church*. Maryknoll, NY: Orbis, 2007.

Wieck, Connie. "Updates from Connie: Where Will Be My Next Teaching Placement?" *Connie's Space*, May 14, 2023. connieinchina.org.

Wilcke, Gerd. "Kellogg to Build 8 Plants in China." *New York Times*, November 28, 1973.

Zehr, Mary Ann. "Chinese Students at IU Back Beijing Protests." *Indianapolis Star*, May 30, 1989.

———. "Chinese Students Grieve for Dead during Memorial Service at IU." *Indianapolis Star*, June 12, 1989.

———. "Chinese Students in U.S. Renounce Ties to Communist Party." *Indianapolis Star*, July 1, 1989.

———. "Chinese Writer Sees Good and Bad in a Changing China." *Herald-Times*, February 2, 1989.

———. "D.C. Rally to Defy Alarms from China." *Indianapolis Star*, May 21, 1989.

———. "Students at Colleges in Indiana Join Rally at Chicago Consulate." *Indianapolis Star*, October 1, 1989.

Zhu, Tianxiao. "Secret Trails: Food and Trade in Late Maoist China, 1960–1978." PhD diss., University of Minnesota, June 2021. ProQuest.